Wanted

Words

**From Armajello to Yawncore —
More Language Gaps Found and Fixed**

Edited by Jane Farrow

**Foreword by Shelagh Rogers
Illustrated by Five Seventeen**

Published in 2001 by
Stoddart Publishing Co. Limited
895 Don Mills Road, 400-2 Park Centre, Toronto, Canada M3C 1W3

www.stoddartpub.com

To order Stoddart books please contact General Distribution Services
Tel. (416) 213-1919   Fax (416) 213-1917

Email cservice@genpub.com

10   9   8   7   6   5   4   3   2   1

National Library of Canada Cataloguing in Publication Data

Main entry under title:
Wanted words 2: from armajello to yawncore: more language gaps found
and fixed

ISBN 0-7737-6232-9

1. English language — New words — Humor.   2. Vocabulary — Humor.
I. Farrow, Jane (Jane Katherine)

PN6231.W64W362   2001   428.1'0207   C2001-901991-2

Cover Design: The Bang
Text design and typesetting: Kinetics Design & Illustration
Illustrations: Five Seventeen

As we put this book together, we tried our best to reach everyone whose ideas
are included. We ask your understanding if we were unable to contact you.

THE CANADA COUNCIL | LE CONSEIL DES ARTS
FOR THE ARTS | DU CANADA
SINCE 1957 | DEPUIS 1957

*We acknowledge for their financial support of our publishing program the Canada Council,
the Ontario Arts Council, and the Government of Canada through the Book Publishing
Industry Development Program (BPIDP).*

Printed and bound in Canada

Wanted
Words
2

Contents

Foreword

It's called "it" — and in my twenty years at CBC Radio, I've been fortunate to work with people like Peter Gzowski, Michael Enright, and Max Ferguson who have "it."

But I knew they had "it" because I had listened to them for years before I ever met them. They were, and are (and to a number, they will hate this), my radio elders. Natural broadcasters. Comfortable in front of the microphone. A sense of mischief. "It" is chemistry, hematology. And Jane Farrow, though she is not my elder, has "it" in spades.

I had heard her engage in badinage with Michael Enright, and frankly, I was just plain jealous. I wanted to play too. And yet, because Jane so "gets" the audience, there was never a moment when I, as a listener, didn't feel included. But I wanted to be right in there in the studio sandbox, spooling out the concoctions of the wordies. Part of my elation at being selected to host "This Morning" was that I would have weekly face time with the woman I called the Pharaoh of Wanted Words.

Man, I was so nervous about that first on-air encounter. Would I be able to play the game? Would I come off as an interloping johnny-come-lately? Could I entertain even the possibility of matching wits with the Pharaoh? To put it more accurately: would my brain keep up with her mouth? At the end of our first session, Jane punched me in the arm and said, "That was fan-TAS-tic. You rock, honey." (I wrote this down in my journal.)

Here's what happens at my end of our encounters. I do the first hour of "This Morning" — usually an issue-oriented story or two about, with luck, topics that are on the minds of the listeners that morning. Then the hour-two theme music starts. I preview what's ahead, concluding with a few teasers from the list of suggestions for the Wanted Word challenge of the week. Every second week, Jane Farrow is preceded by the brilliant Jane Kansas (who also has "it"), our regular contributor from Nova Scotia. I like to call that blissful block of the program the all-Jane half-hour.

Jane Farrow comes into the studio during a cut of music. Do you wonder, as I did, what she looks like? Well, she's medium-tall, with Tintin-like brown hair. She usually wears a short-sleeved shirt, and invariably it has a name tag above the breast pocket (because, also invariably, it is part of a uniform for a bowling league or the family mechanic down the street). Jane's hands when she talks resemble those of a great conductor — she shapes phrases with her hands. And like a great conductor, she knows that silence is as important on radio as sound. She'll let things hang in the air sometimes. Usually when she's waiting for me to get the joke.

So we've got her in the studio and you know about her gestures. We start off with my reading the mail (a great tradition in the nine-to-noontime slot) from the wordies.

For instance, a letter from Jeff Chang in Calgary, in response to the challenge of what to call the saggy underside of the upper arm, had us in stitches. Jeff coined a word based on his memories of his school music teacher, Mrs. Sterling, leading the class in song. "The skin on her upper arms hung low and swung rhythmically as she jabbed the air with her baton . . . [reminding] me of a pendulum. Therefore my suggestion for this Wanted Word is 'pendularm.'" The wordies' letters are fabulous.

Okay. Then it's on to the short list of suggestions. We read them and try really hard to pronounce the names of the wordies' home towns. Then it's time to pick the five winners. This is tough. And the Pharaoh and I don't always agree. I am a sucker for a truly sick pun. Jane loves the words that involve lateral thinking. I think that, between us, there's a good balance.

The winners are announced, followed by the Wanted Word challenge for the next week, the ways to reach us, and the goodbyes, and Jane exits stage left. What happens when Jane leaves? There's less oxygen in the room.

In truth, words fail me. What I can tell you is what you already know or you wouldn't have this book before you now. Jane Farrow is an intuitive broadcaster. She has connected with you. She is the "it" girl. And it's a sheer pleasure for me to be party to Wanted Words.

— Shelagh Rogers, host of "This Morning"

Introduction

Well, ain't life grand. I have the pleasure of writing the introduction to another *Wanted Words* book (the one you're now holding in your hands), and you're about to plunge into the collective genius of Canada's hitherto unsung lexicographers. I'm happy to say that the wordies, as I've come to call them, have outdone themselves this time. Their brilliant creations continue to amaze all who catch the weekly Wanted Words segment on CBC Radio One's "This Morning." But the big news is that *Wanted Words* (the first volume) made the leap from radio wave to printed page with a spectacular eighteen-week run on the national best-seller lists. Wordies, take a bow!

As far as I can tell, the popularity of Wanted Words directly relates to the joy we all take in playing with language. The creative wordsmiths you'll encounter in these pages are adventurous and curious; they refuse to be hemmed in by the bow-tied conventions of our lexicon. Faced with a gap in the language, wordies simply concoct something brilliant on the spot.

Over the two years I've been doing Wanted Words, I've

enjoyed getting to know some of the people behind these freshly minted expressions. I admire their smarts in coming up with the words, as well as their determination to contribute in the face of stiff competition. This book even provided me with a perfect excuse to work the crowd at a few CBC events and book signings and meet some wordies in the flesh. I am honoured by the esteem and respect with which this modest word game, and CBC Radio in general, is held.

The 400 to 1,500 Wanted Words letters, e-mails, and faxes I got to read each Wednesday were the highlight of my workweek. The wordies often shared stories about personal foibles or eccentricities that were hilarious and painfully honest. We've reprinted some here in these pages, and I hope you enjoy reading them as much as I did. I was delighted and sometimes quite moved to learn how the game was modified and played among friends and families — Wanted Words, it seems, helped pass the time during boring drives and commutes; it enlivened dinner parties; it was a big hit at an annual street-hockey party; and it was a light-hearted way for an ailing father and his doting daughter to keep in touch while living in different cities.

The hardest part of my Wanted Words duties was determining, in the case of duplicate entries, which nimble and quick wordsmith got his or her creation across the finish line first. I had to resort to a means test I called "the surface-mail regional co-efficient." Basically, I magically readjusted time and space to give a boost to Westerners and snail-mail holdouts, who were at a disadvantage to those wordies with e-mail and, if they lived in the East, up to a four-hour head start.

I thank you all for making Wanted Words a wonderful segment to produce and present. And that goes for everyone who's ever submitted a word, as well as for those who quietly enjoy them or invent them for their own amusement. I encourage you to use them in daily speech, whether you're a **leaderhoser** or you like to **bedic** on Monday mornings. Maybe we'll all share a big yuk when one of them ends up in the *Oxford*.

And now a word about the host of "This Morning," Shelagh Rogers. People often ask me what's she really like. I tell them it's quite simple — what you hear is what you get. She's kind, generous, brilliant, funny, patient, persistent, charismatic, and spectacularly humble. Walking into Shelagh's natural habitat, CBC studio 322, is like entering a tropical jungle — it's all lush, warm, and totally inviting. Shelagh makes you feel so utterly comfortable and welcome in her studio that you can, quite literally, forget there are a couple of microphones between you. And that a million or so people are listening in on your conversation. Ms. Rogers has that rare gift of making people feel that they belong, that their contribution is not only needed, but also brilliantly conceived. You could call her an invisible leader; she's someone who has heaps of integrity and leads not by directive, but by example and encouragement. Her talents and charms are a source of inspiration for all of us at "This Morning" — and that includes her ability to execute a perfect cannonball at the staff pool party. Thanks a bunch, Sheel.

I have some behind-the-scenes folks to thank too. They're the ones who make the Wanted Words show and books possible. First up, Ira Basen, my number-one Wanted Words

editor, ideas man, and mentor. You may recognize his name
from the show credits of any number of CBC Radio programs
he's helped create and produce (including "Workology," the
summer series I hosted), but I know him simply as "boss" —
and I'll tell you, he's one of the funniest, smartest, most
gruelling of the bunch. His impossibly high standards are
both a blessing and a curse, and somewhere along the line,
they earned him the handle "the Human Bottleneck" — a
moniker he continues to earn on a daily basis. But really,
what more could you ask for in a boss? He might make you
rewrite a piece six times and perform it a dozen more to get
it right, but when he finally does sign off on it, you can be
sure it's paydirt.

My researcher and fellow radio producer, Marta Saunders,
has acted as chief wrangler for this volume of *Wanted Words*,
and she has done a bang-up job keeping it all together,
chasing down people and facts, and just generally being (this
will make her cringe) wonderful. Lisa Ayuso does support
work at "This Morning," and as my long-term Wanted Words
deputy, she keeps me focused, sane, and frequently in
stitches. I never thank her enough (because it makes her
cringe as well), but here it is in print, missy. Oh, and did I
mention that Lisa introduced us to our gifted illustrator, Five
Seventeen? I am so proud of his work here. He has taken
these words to a whole other level with his awesome and
frequently hilarious drawings. Good work, team!

My "This Morning" co-workers continue to be a reliable
source of support and inspiration, as do my desk editors and
the executive producer, Susan Mahoney, Marie Clarke, and
Judy MacAlpine. I also want to thank all the wickedly sharp

radio hosts I've had fun with along the way, including
Michael Enright, Dick Gordon, and Ralph Benmergui.

Finally, I am grateful to my talented copy editor, Janice
Weaver. Whew, what an eye for detail. It's been a delight
working with everyone at Stoddart Publishing, from top to
bottom. They've done a great job of pulling both books
together, packaging them, selling them, and shipping them
out. Thanks to Terry Palmer, Sue Sumeraj, Simon Ware,
Don Bastian, Nelson Doucet, and Bill Douglas. Oh, and even
though she's not on the payroll at Stoddart or the CBC, I
want to thank Sophie Hackett for being my daily source of
heart-and-soul jet fuel.

Now turn the page — it's time to expand your vocabulary!

— Jane Farrow

Armajello

Noun:

the saggy underside of the upper arm, commonly found on ageing adults.

Submitted by Jeanette Page, Rosedale Valley, Alberta

Most folks lose the elastic recoil in their skin after the age of forty. Our skin and tendons just don't snap back

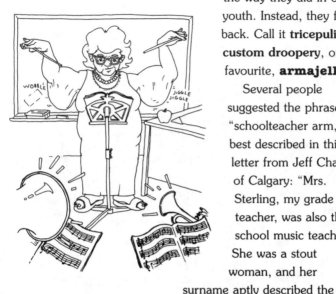

the way they did in our youth. Instead, they flap back. Call it **tricepulite**, **custom droopery**, or our favourite, **armajello**.

Several people suggested the phrase "schoolteacher arm," best described in this letter from Jeff Chang of Calgary: "Mrs. Sterling, my grade 3 teacher, was also the school music teacher. She was a stout woman, and her surname aptly described the colour of her hair. She conducted music vigorously when she led us in songs like 'Three Jolly Blacksmiths.' The skin on her upper arms hung low and swung rhythmically as she jabbed the air with her baton. The low-hanging skin reminded me of a pendulum. Therefore, my suggestion for this Wanted Word is 'pendularm.'"

Here is a short list of words honouring this hitherto unnamed body part:

- **armadreadin** — Don Kennedy, Goulais River, Ontario
- **armlobe** — Raef and Val Wilson, Fletchers Lake, Nova Scotia

- **armwattle** — Michael Evans, Port Perry, Ontario
- **batwing** — Doug Bremner, Dundas, Ontario
- **bingo-arm** — Sandy Thorburn, Toronto
- **bisag** — Nicola Hamer, Ottawa
- **chickwing** — Anne King, Brantford, Ontario
- **custom droopery** — Mike Godin, Pembroke, Ontario
- **flabcep** — Melanie Flanagan, Barnaby River, New Brunswick
- **flopcep** — Céline Papillon and Maurice Strasfeld, New Glasgow, Nova Scotia
- **hen-hock** — Randy McNally, Aroostook, New Brunswick
- **pelican arm** — Roy Olynick, West St. Paul, Manitoba
- **sagcep** — Jean Lyle, Brighton, Ontario
- **tricepulite** — Robert Scott, Saint John
- **trisag** — Don and Joan Lyons, Kamloops, British Columbia
- **trislop** — Shannon Fair, Kamloops, British Columbia
- **udderarm** — Arthur Entlich, Victoria
- **wattle wings** — Trevor Shpeley, Kelowna, British Columbia
- **wing flab** — Marlene Jones, Victoria

B

Baton Rude

Noun:

the plastic bar used to divide
shoppers' groceries at the checkout counter.
Submitted by Pam and Rodney Graham, Richibucto,
New Brunswick

Some Wanted Word challenges arrive in small, perfectly formed queries, like this one from Michael Eisen of Ottawa: "We need a name for that plastic bar thing that divides my groceries from those of the person next to me. Everyone uses these things religiously to distance my bread and eggs from my neighbour's milk. What gives?"

It sounded simple enough. But we soon found out the checkout conveyor was a tinderbox that, when ignited by the **grubstake**, would explode into flames of impassioned debate (see letters below). Some people put the **condimental divide** in the Most Useful Objects Hall of Fame, right up there with safety pins and mousetraps. They claim it's a common courtesy, and saves time and worry. Others aren't convinced of its charms. They resent the anti-social implications of the **baton rude**, and feel like they're slamming a door in their neighbour's face when they bang it down on the checkout conveyor.

Here are some other clever suggestions:

- **back-off bar** — J. L. Bond, Steinbach, Manitoba
- **the checkout Charlie** — Paul Ojalammi, Sudbury, Ontario
- **clerk preserver** — Genevieve Willis, Ottawa
- **the condimental divide** — David and Gillian Calder, Vancouver
- **foobar** — Andrew Rivett, St. Catharines, Ontario
- **food fence** — Harold Hoglund, Constance Bay, Ontario
- **foodfender** — Paul Pasternak, Powell River, British Columbia
- **the grape divide** — Kay Bannard, Calgary
- **grocery gate** — Amy Taylor, Muskoka, Ontario

- **grubclub** — Irwin Friesen, North Battleford, Saskatchewan
- **grubguard** — Donna Sheppard, Prince George, British Columbia
- **grubstake** — Shirley Ring, Seaforth, Ontario
- **jar bar** — Jody Seguin, Fort St. John, British Columbia
- **mineline** — Andrew Neale, Victoria
- **orderborder** — Joan Stephens, Campbell River, British Columbia
- **provision division** — Don Dougherty, Halifax
- **shopstick** — Lorna Rosell, Calgary
- **talliwacker** — James Hillier, Vancouver
- **vittlestick** — Ron Butler, South Slocan, British Columbia

The **grape divide** has some people feeling guilty, while others claim they can't offload their shopping cart without it. Here to make the case "for" the **food fence** is shopper Gail Norcross of Vancouver: "I find standing in line at the grocery checkout irritating enough without having to watch my groceries to make sure they go home with me and not with the person in front of me or behind me. Also, I don't want their stuff. I slam down that plastic bar thing if the person in front of me doesn't. I've always viewed using [it] as a considerate thing to do for the person coming after me, [and] now I hear it makes me a social misfit! Well, so be it. However, I have noticed that those men who don't eat quiche also don't do the plastic bar thing . . . A generalization, I know, but one arising from many, many grocery checkout experiences."

There were many listeners ready to make the case "against" **foobars**. Carol Shaw of Shawnigan Lake, British Columbia, for example, had a pretty negative experience with the

grubstake. "The other day I plunked down my five-pound bag of potatoes, a litre of milk, and a loaf of bread at the register. A middle-aged woman behind me became flustered and pointedly placed 'her' bar after my food items. But she didn't stop there. She then proceeded to place another bar at the *beginning* of my groceries. Reaching across and in front of me in a most melodramatic way, she dropped the bar from six inches in the air to drive her point home. As you can imagine, I'm not an avid fan."

But really, this small piece of plastic points to the larger phenomenon of negotiating personal space in an impersonal world. Heather Graham of Victoria wrote, "I think you miss the point by focusing on the sticks themselves rather than on what they are doing: defining someone's space entitlement in a situation where space is a scarce resource. The sticks are doing the same thing that parking lines and even parking meters do — telling you how much room your car is entitled to take up in the parking lot or on the street. Or how about theatre and airplane seats? The arms aren't there just so you have somewhere to rest your elbows; they also tell the people on either side of you where their space entitlement stops and yours starts. Space defining is an important element in lessening social anxiety. It also lessens personal stress. In the case of the checkout lineup, it means that shoppers don't have to watch what's going on; they can keep an eye on the kids, glance through a magazine, or just relax. The cashier doesn't have to guess or ask questions to know who's buying what. And it also allows people to perform one of those nice little courtesies for each other in passing the stick along the line."

But who really matters in all this? The cashiers. We heard from several of them, including Genevieve Willis of Ottawa. "Having worked many years as a retail cashier, grocery and otherwise," she wrote, "I find the bar's function obvious — and it's not anti-social. After several hours of pushing various food items over an electronic scanning device, the hapless clerk cannot easily distinguish which groceries belong to which customer. And sometimes it gets nasty. If the cashier mistakenly grabs the next customer's L'il Debbie snack cakes or tube of Squeez Cheez, he/she will be greeted by a glare and a haughty 'That's not mine!' (read: 'How could you be so stupid as to think that I would be purchasing that?'). The fewer of these unpleasant interactions the clerk has to face during a long shift, in a largely thankless and mechanically repetitive service-industry job, the better. I am sure that anyone who has worked on the other side of the retail machine would be inclined, at least in their darker moments, to agree with me. I therefore suggest 'clerk preserver' as an adequate description for the redemptive function of the much-maligned little plastic grocery bar."

Beditate

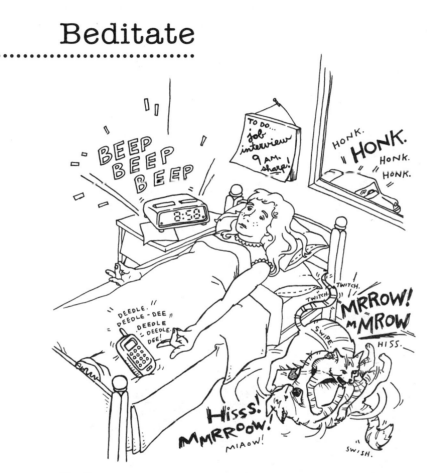

Verb:

the act of lying down, tuning out, and letting
your mind drift, usually done in bed in the morning.
Submitted by John O'Byrne, Dublin, Ireland

Beditating is an intensely meditative and relaxing experience. It's really quite simple: you lie or lounge in a bed, in a comfy chair, or on a couch and do nothing but space out. On a good day, a few moments of **loungevity** can stretch into a blissful hour or two.

Beditating is not the same thing as stressing out, fretting, or napping. And it should not be confused with lying in bed listening to the radio or reading. The sad thing is, **beditating** is often accompanied by the nagging guilt trip that we should be up and doing something "productive." Marsha Williams of Victoria cherishes her **mornopause** and gets around some of the guilty feelings this way: "I call it 'lateral sinking.' It happens a lot on dark and dreary mornings. At five-minute intervals, I figure out what else I can leave off the list in order to extend the lie-in:

- 'Hey! I just had a shower yesterday!'
- 'Breakfast is a highly overrated meal anyway.'
- 'No point ironing that shirt really — it'll just get wrinkled.'
- 'My hair is shiny, not greasy.'"

We think the world would be a better place if we laid in a little longer each morning, but if **beditating** doesn't work for you, seek out your own comfort level with some of these words:

- **calm-a-sutra** — John O'Byrne, Dublin, Ireland
- **consciousness objector** — John Lund, London, Ontario
- **futonics** — Anya MacLeod, Vancouver

- **horizontal hold** — Steve Peters, Gloucester, Ontario
- **loungevity** — Frances Buchan, Prince Albert, Saskatchewan
- **morning stickness** — Margaret Hampshire, Terrace, British Columbia
- **morningslide** — Ray Lees, Ottawa
- **mornopause** — Mayfair Sign Crew, Chilliwack, British Columbia
- **postproning** — Pamela Legg, Pemberton, British Columbia
- **procouchinate** — Ann Turcke, Kingston, Ontario
- **procrashtinate** — Luci Dickerson, Pembroke, Ontario
- **procrastilazing** — Roger Sturtevant, Clementsport, Nova Scotia
- **procrastinertia** — Adrian Cooper, Kingston, Ontario
- **quilt trip** — Richard Frost, Windsor, Ontario
- **quilty pleasure** — Kim Dunn, Bedford, Nova Scotia
- **rigormattress** — Mike and Cheryl Baxter, London, Ontario
- **slouch potato** — Janet Heaven
- **staydreamer** — Tim Storey, Cormac, Ontario
- **upnertia** — Chris McLean, Revelstoke, British Columbia

According to Angie Stevens of Quebec City, homo sapiens were not the first creatures to master **beditating**. Ever since learning about primates at university, she's been calling this behaviour "doing the orangutan." As she explained, "Orangutans build a nest of leaves and branches in the treetops each night for sleeping. They wake up very early in the morning, but they lounge in their nests for hours on end before getting up. Picture a huge orangutan lazing about, occasionally reaching out for a fresh leaf to chew on or shifting [his] weight for [his] morning toilet routine. They are truly the champions of bed lounging."

Staying with the primate theme but moving up the evolutionary ladder to homo sapiens, Anya MacLeod of Vancouver offers this ode to the act of **beditating**: "I well know that feeling of lying in my toasty bed with my cat sprawled on my feet and a concert of alarms going off around me (I have three). Long ago, a kindred soul and I came up with the term 'sandboxing' for being in bed doing nothing in particular, and it has always seemed apt to me. Like kids who kinda aimlessly move sand around, I can easily just lie in bed for hours, letting my little mind merrily trip along in no foreseeable direction. Heaven. However, that is a weekend/holiday term. During the week, when I absolutely do not want to get out of bed to go to work, I belinger (malinger + bed) till the last possible minute or indulge in some futonics (a.k.a. reality-wrestling) in bed. Lord, why aren't we just allowed to hibernate during these bleak winter months, with time-outs for snowboarding and hot mulled wine?"

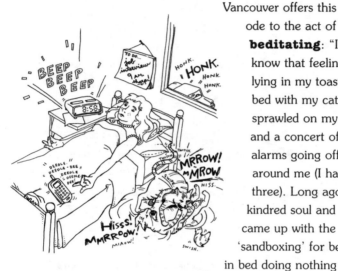

Blabrynth

Noun:
the elaborate maze of voicemail
menus and prompts encountered when
phoning businesses or government offices.

Submitted by Jack Brady, Gore Bay, Ontario

Once upon a time, in a land much like our own, phone calls were answered by human beings. The exchange went something like this:

Receptionist: Acme Screw and Gear, may I help you?
Caller: Yes, may I speak to Miss Dingle, please?
Receptionist: Certainly. Let me connect you.

That was it! Within seconds, you and Miss Dingle were making beautiful noise together. Today, you are more likely to hear something like this: "Welcome to the Acme Screw and Gear voicemail system. We are pleased to present you with the following menu of options. If you are calling from a touch-tone phone, press 1 now. If you know the name of the party you are trying to reach, press 2 now . . . Welcome to the Acme Screw and Gear staff directory. If you know the last name of the party you are trying to reach, please begin spelling the name now."

Sound familiar? Welcome to the world of the **blabrynth** — a black hole of voicemail commands from which you can pound and pound, and never escape. And it is only getting worse. The voicemail wardens continue to perfect the **voicemail jail**, adding new off-ramps and sealing up easy escape routes (like pressing zero to scoot ahead to a real human). And the worthy caller who finally arrives at his chosen destination is often subjected to the cruel fate of excruciating corporate jingles or easy-listening versions of Nirvana's "Smells Like Teen Spirit." This is **Alexander Graham hell**, an infernal place to which you are condemned for the crime of trying to talk to another human being.

- **abysmail** — Ken Smyth, Sault Ste. Marie, Ontario
- **Alexander Graham hell** — Al Loeppky, Winkler, Manitoba
- **bell jar** — Ian Milligan, Waterloo, Ontario
- **blabberynth** — Robert Wilson, Dauphin, Manitoba
- **cataphones** — Hilary Tyler, Trenton, Ontario
- **lost and pound** — Kerry Daly, Guelph, Ontario
- **telabyss** — Alice Morin, Regina
- **telehell** — Eron Main, Ottawa
- **telemaze** — Rosemary Batchilder, Georgetown, Prince Edward Island
- **teletrap** — Bob McLarty, Ottawa
- **twilight phone** — Greg Long, Washago, Ontario
- **voice jail** — Margaret Christakos, Toronto
- **voicemail jail** — Tyler Caughill, Sault Ste. Marie, Ontario
- **voicemaze** — Jolan Canrinus, Toronto, and Bev Hummitzsch, King City, Ontario
- **voitex** — Emma Levez, Powell River, British Columbia
- **vox hole** — Lisa Sharpe, Cranbrook, British Columbia
- **voxtrap** — Joyce Boon, Kelowna, British Columbia

Bootroute

Noun:

a narrow path cut through snow or
snowbanks, approximately the width of one boot.

Submitted by Deborah Turney Zagwyn, Harrison Hot Springs,
British Columbia

When it comes to blazing trails through the snow, Canadians set a high standard. We can plough, sweep, and shovel with the best of them, but there are times when we simply have to tough it out on the **chillboot pass**. The **bootroute** is more than a set of footprints, however; it's a treacherous winter footpath that calls for heightened navigational skills, steady balance, and finely honed negotiating skills (to be used when encountering other travellers on the **Snow Chi Minh trail**).

You'll find **bootroutes** on city sidewalks where the property owner hasn't shovelled. You'll find them in parks where people like to take a winter stroll, but the city workers never plough. Some of them are clean and fresh; some of them are blackened by sludge and muck. Real Canadians know how to perform the **slidewalk**. It's just another way that we refuse to allow winter to get the upper hand.

- **bootchute** — Warren Graham, Toronto
- **bootrack** — Beverly Kerr, Montreal
- **chillboot pass** — Todd Yaschuk, Hammonds Plains, Nova Scotia
- **cold cuts** — Susan Bithrey, Thunder Bay, Ontario
- **crevath** — Peter Howe, Ottawa
- **freezeway** — Niki Spourgitis, London, Ontario
- **galoshgroove** — Happy Mireault, Cobourg, Ontario
- **ididarut** — Susan Chapman, Napanee, Ontario
- **precipass** — Barbara DuTot, Enderby, British Columbia
- **slidewalk** — Dave O'Hearn, Marysville, Ontario
- **slushcut** — Ian and Debbie Wrong, Toronto
- **snevice** — Deborah Rose, Mount Forest, Ontario

- **Snow Chi Minh trail** — Pieter Blokker, Kingston, Ontario
- **snoway** — Olivier Fuldauer, Calgary
- **strugglers' notch** — Kris Kiviaho, Elliot Lake, Ontario

We were also intrigued by these suggestions: **Wenceslas way**, suggested by Shirley and Larry Allen of Cambridge, Ontario, and **Wencespath**, submitted by Joe Robson of North Sydney, Nova Scotia. To be honest, the connection between the legendary good king and the **bootroute** had never occurred to us. But now that we've delved into this a little deeper, it makes a lot of sense.

You may recall the story. King Wenceslas looks out his window on the Feast of Stephen and sees a peasant collecting fuel for the winter. He decides he will join him back at his place, a league or so away. Being the king, he doesn't travel alone, and he tells his page, "Bring me flesh, bring me wine; we're going on a road trip." They set out in a raging snowstorm, with the page leading the way. After a few miles, the page tires out and can't go any farther. King Wenceslas digs deep and offers to blaze the **bootroute** for his page with these immortal words:

"Mark my footsteps, my good page,
Tread thou in them boldly:
Thou shalt find the winter's rage
Freeze thy blood less coldly."

In his master's steps he trod,
Where the snow lay dinted;
Heat was in the very sod
Which the Saint had printed.

Therefore, Christian men, be sure,
Wealth or rank possessing,
Ye who now will bless the poor,
Shall yourselves find blessing.

So there you have it. After carefully reviewing the evidence, we are now ready to proclaim King Wenceslas the patron saint of the **bootroute**, even though he's not a Canadian.

Bragrag

Noun:

the form letter families send out around Christmastime
to boast about their travels, social triumphs, and career
accomplishments.

Submitted by Annette Van Grootheest, Drayton, Ontario

We love Wanted Words because we never know when we are going to strike a nerve. For example, when we asked listeners for a name for those family form letters that people like to send around at Christmastime, we had no idea that we were going to uncover such a rich vein of pent-up anger and resentment.

These **conceitsheets** seem harmless enough — an opportunity to allow family and friends to catch up with the news of the past year — but our listeners know that a much more sinister purpose lurks just below that smarmy surface. Remember little Johnny? He's been accepted to Harvard — at age sixteen! And little Debbie, who used to sing those lovely Christmas carols at the church every year? Why, she's now being wooed by the Canadian Opera Company. And baby Kimmi? She's all of four and able to paddle her own kayak through river rapids! The best news is that clever Roger bought Nortel at $10 and sold at $110.

Get the message? Your life might suck, but ours is *perfect*!

Some people defended the **bragna carta** on the grounds that it is an efficient way to stay in touch. And a few even sent us some pretty entertaining alternatives to the **brag rag**: "Blake lost another club championship. We all struggled through three agonizing weeks of his athletic humiliation and self-loathing. When he finally smiled again, there was mould on his teeth."

Gary Brown of Colonsay, Saskatchewan, spotted this missing word. Here are some of the wonderful suggestions submitted by our extraordinary listeners (and we're not bragging!):

- **better-letter** — Melissa Chapman, Oshawa, Ontario
- **boast post** — Mary Robinson, Fredericton
- **boast-it note** — Tony and Maureen Simmonds, Powell River, British Columbia
- **borrespondence** — Mark Shields, Queen Charlotte Islands, British Columbia
- **bragalogue** — Ria Meronek, Calgary
- **bragitorial** — Jenny Day, Keswick, Ontario
- **the bragna carta** — Shannon Liston, London, Ontario
- **conceitsheet** — Greg and Charmaine Derksen, Surrey, British Columbia
- **famail** — Corina Dootjes, Canmore, Alberta
- **famspam** — Isabel Fonte, Montreal
- **gloatnote** — Joan Lyons, Kamloops, British Columbia
- **mailbrag** — Jackie Avent, Winnipeg
- **me-mail** — Bob Waldon, Alert Bay, British Columbia
- **oozeletter** — Nick Tinker, Nepean, Ontario

We received many wonderful letters on this challenge. Melissa Chapman of Oshawa, Ontario, fantasized about the reply she will probably never send: "Thank you for the card, but please don't send them any more. I can't help but notice that your life is many times more interesting than my own, and I feel small and uninteresting when I consider how many trips to Iceland I did not make this year. I just can't bring myself to compose one of these better-letters, in which we would boast of our achievements: changed over one thousand diapers, walked the dog, shovelled the snow, made many, many okay-tasting dinners, took frequent trips to the corner store, saw two movies, and shampooed the carpet last spring."

And here's one from Fiona Stevenson of Ottawa, who
finds herself the unwilling subject of the family **bragrag**:
"I don't know who started it in my father's family, but now his
brothers send a Christmas brag letter, each trying to outbrag
the other. These letters are extraordinary for their magical
ability to make our dull lives sound somehow exceptional.
I like to think of myself as a kind of muse for my father, who
each year has to find a new and interesting way of telling the
family that I am not getting married, don't own a new house
or have a new job, didn't travel anywhere or win anything.
I know my simple life drives him to greater imaginative depths
than Charles Dickens himself in an attempt to squeeze a good
brag out of it. I can't wait to see the mental gymnastics he
will perform this year!"

Ted Adel is a letter carrier in Whitehorse. He wrote,
"Today the temperature hovered at -30°C. It occurred to me
that the overflowing mail bag that I was about to hoist onto
my shoulder contained many of those larger-than-life, too-
good-to-be-true, oh-so-cute seasonal newsletters. I suppose
we could make the Wanted Word national and refer to it
as 'Canada Boast' — all hand-delivered by frozen posties
everywhere."

Cancuffs

Noun:

the plastic ring that holds together six-packs of beer or pop.

Submitted by Kevin Robart, Moncton, New Brunswick

Most of the time on Wanted Words, we are trying to fill a gap that exists in the language. But there are occasions when our mission is simply to improve on what is already there. Take the case of so-called rim-applied carriers. You may think these are aircraft carriers stationed in the Pacific Rim. Or bicycle baskets fastened above the wheels. But you would probably never guess that they're those plastic rings that bind together six-packs.

It's true! "Rim-applied carriers" is the official name used by the beverage industry. Kind of sad, isn't it! Compare that to **drink-link**, **brew bra**, **cannector**, or our favourite, **cancuffs**, and you'll realize what a valuable service Wanted Words provides every week.

Now, the good news about **cancuffs** is that they fit nicely between your fingers and swing a little like a bowling ball when you walk. The bad news is that they are dangerous to fish and waterfowl. The beverage industry reports that in Canada, six-packs are giving way to cardboard-wrapped twelve- and twenty-four-packs. In the meantime, here's a tip to the fowl-friendly: snip the **goosenoose** with scissors before disposing of it.

And heeeeere's the short list:

- **brew bra** — Phil Smith, Ucluelet, British Columbia
- **cancollar** — Farid Rashid, Toronto
- **canhandle** — Gaye Squires, Dartmouth, Nova Scotia
- **canloops** — Jaimes Joshko, Victoria
- **cannector** — Dave Rowley, Maple Creek, Saskatchewan
- **canoose** — Inez Lazzari and Jim Haines, Thunder Bay, Ontario

- **can-span** — Chris Morrison, Ontario
- **choke-a-cola** — Laird Hurley, Toronto
- **drink-link** — Lesley Levy, Montreal
- **goosenoose** — Shirley Osterman, Sarnia, Ontario
- **guzzlemuzzle** — Muriel Goldston, Sydney, Nova Scotia
- **hexagrabber** — Linda Landry, Ottawa
- **quackrack** — Sandy Strunk, Richmond, Virginia
- **six sling** — Janet Stein, Edmonton
- **six-pack Cadillac** — Patrice Lyon, Laurel, Ontario

Leave it to the craftier among us to come up with the ultimate use for the **brew bra**. Sandy van Laar of Creemore, Ontario, wrote: "As a snowbird in Florida, my husband observed a charming use for these cancuffs — they make lovely plastic lawn hyacinths. Just cut them up into single circles and layer them on wire coat hangers. Spray paint them bright colours and display on the front lawn — beautiful for any winter garden!"

Wait, there's more! Candace Cowan of Errington, British Columbia, says she's seen **cancuffs** made into Christmas snowflakes with the aid of a stapler and some sparkles. Add a few cement dwarfs and a plywood cut-out of a young child peeing into the tulips, and you have a front lawn gallery that will make you the envy of the neighbourhood.

Cherishable

Noun:

a wanted gift that the receiver can't bring him- or herself to use.

Submitted by Serena Martindale, Calgary

There's the gift that won't stop giving, and then there's the **cherishable** — the gift that won't *start* giving. **Cherishables** are gifts that you actually want, even yearn for, but can't bring yourself to use. They are usually luxury goods like scented candles, expensive salad oils, toiletries, linens, high-end golf balls, or a piece of clothing that is simply too good to be worn.

Cherishables are not gifts that are being hoarded; rather, they are **ever-presents** that are protected, often in museum condition, from the rigours of the everyday use for which they are intended. Using a **sentimento** would somehow jeopardize all the love and affection it embodies. **Cherishables** are almost always being saved for a special occasion that never arrives. The owners of these **reapsakes** have been known to invest considerable energy in preserving and maintaining their gift museum, sometimes by doing things like keeping soaps and candles dust-free with the aid of a blow-dryer.

And now, luxuriate in some of these precious coinages:

- **ever-present** — Sandy Laurikainen, Hinton, Alberta
- **luxuria** — Paul Kocak, Syracuse, New York
- **magpiler** — Ted Cavanagh and Alison Evans, Halifax
- **petrigift** — Geoffrey Oliver, Ottawa
- **presentimento** — Julia Rowlands, Ottawa
- **reapsake** — Beverley Rook, Oakville, Ontario
- **savouries** — Susan Freedman, Vancouver
- **sentimento** — Talia Goldstein, Geraldton, Ontario
- **sinventory** — Victoria Warford, St. John's
- **use-me-not** — Marc Gareau, London, Ontario
- **weepsake** — Charles Follini, Fredericton

Independent of one another, Margret Huntley of Victoria
and Edwina Faith Elliott of Ottawa both spotted this void in
the language. **Cherishables** draw on people's urge to
conserve, which is closely linked to their undying inability to
pamper themselves. This often stems from their experiences
growing up in a world of scarcity.

We received this letter from Richard Miklenic of Tofino,
British Columbia. "I was born in Canada and grew up with
a lot of people who had endured the Second World War," he
wrote. "Most had endured the ravages of child poverty before
that. They are very generous people like my grandmother,
who still lives as if the war might come back. Things given
to them often end up being stockpiled in closets for a special
occasion that rarely, if ever, arrives. I have often said to her,
'Granny, why don't you pull that fancy tea set out of the
closet and use it?' 'Oh no, I can't do that. It's much too nice,
and besides, it's a present from you.' It is sad that they can't
allow themselves to enjoy the things that, at one time, they
could only dream of having. I call these gifts 'keepsafes.'"

Christopher Earls of Des Ruisseaux, Quebec, proposed
that the person who can't use new gifts be called a neo-
phobe. He suggested the following cure: "One method of
reducing the anxiety is to submit the item to a process that
I call ripening. Ripening consists of allowing the item in
question to sit on a shelf, hanger, or in a dresser drawer for
a period of six months to several years. Generally, the object
is usable after this ripening period. Severe sufferers of neo-
phobia experience anxiety, discomfort, and vague feelings of
guilt when they themselves purchase an item and are forced
to use it immediately. We usually purchase an item, scurry

home, and quickly hide it — hoping that no one will discover it before the ripening process is complete."

The ripening manoeuvre unavoidably introduces the unsavoury possibility of over-ripening. This happened to Maria Edelman of St. Catharines, Ontario, with a **sentimento** she bought for herself some time ago. "Many, many years ago, I treated myself to an expensive pair of shoes. A lovely pair of shoes. A gorgeous pair of shoes. Brown and beige and burgundy straps on low, comfortable heels — a real find. I loved them so much I decided to wear them only on special occasions. Every so often, I would take them out of the box and admire them and put them back in again, waiting for that special occasion. Many years passed. And then last year, a distant niece invited me to her wedding. I decided the time had come. The shoes complemented my outfit perfectly. I felt good and strode confidently out of the parking lot. And stumbled slightly. My shoes seemed to be sticking to the pavement. Thinking I had stepped on some gum, I scraped them off and continued walking. And stumbled again. And scraped again. The stickiness persisted. Deciding to take a better look at this offending substance, I took off my shoes — and gazed in horror at the cracks and crevices distorting my pristine soles. The soles of the precious shoes were disintegrating on my feet, leaving a trail of crumbly goo. By the end of the day, my stride had become a stagger and my shoes were in shreds."

Copychat

Verb:

to adopt the accent of strangers or
companions with whom one is speaking.

Submitted by Maire McDermott, Winnipeg

What is it about drinking a Guinness that makes a person go all lilty and Irish? Or who can explain the Canadian who sounds all Scandinavian while shopping at Ikea? And let's not forget the overeager host who feels it is a supreme act of hospitality to mimic his guest's accent. But before we get too uppity about **copychatters** and their **accentuaping** ways, we should all try saying, "Captain Kirk, we cannot hold her at warp five much longer," without adopting the distinctive brogue of *Star Trek*'s Scottie.

Accents have an infectious quality, and that's what the **copychatter** can't resist. **Shadowvoxing** is an innocent enough attempt at immersing oneself in someone else's world, but taken out of context, it sounds pompous and inane. Like ordering a "spot o' tea" at Tim Hortons.

This gap in the lexicon was spotted by Erin Pettit and Talin Vartanian of Toronto. Please feel free to adopt any accent you like when pronouncing these new additions to the language:

- **accentricity** — Darren Miller, Grande Prairie, Alberta
- **accentuape** — Bruce Nunn, Halifax
- **chameleovox** — Marilyn Junk, Mississauga, Ontario
- **copyglot** — Sue Donaldson, Perth, Ontario
- **dittolect** — Brian Higdon, Corner Brook, Newfoundland
- **echolocution** — Bob Sidebotham, Langley, British Columbia
- **idiomsyncratic** — Anne-Marie Jennings, Inuvik, Northwest Territories
- **imitalk** — Carolyn Hayes, Corner Brook, Newfoundland
- **moccent** — Lynn Senecal, Montreal

- **mocktalk** — Alexandra Haagaard, Port Perry, Ontario
- **morphonics** — Jill Nielsen, Cambridge, Ontario
- **shadowvox** — Denise Hay, London, Ontario
- **sympatois** — Patrick Gage, Nanaimo, British Columbia
- **voicemosis** — John Cavacuiti, Vancouver
- **voissimilate** — Ken Babich, Saskatoon
- **vox copuli** — Kevin Brennan, Fredericton
- **voxmosis** — Hoi Kong, Montreal

Lots of people freely admitted to practising **voxmosis,**
like Bethe Wettlaufer of Woodstock, Ontario. "My word for
innocently copying other people's accents is 'echoidiom,'"
she wrote. "This happened to me when I stayed with friends
in Georgia for two weeks. Not only did I develop a sugary
southern drawl, I started using some of their phrases. When
I returned home, I received a puzzled look from my mother
when I told her I was 'fixing to hug her.'"

Then there's the accent that turns the corner into
stereotyping and becomes an insult. That's not always what
the speaker thinks he's doing, but innocent bystanders may
cringe and think otherwise. Dijana McNicoll of Calgary wrote
this letter about her husband: "My spouse baffles and enrages
me every time he starts sliding down the smooth and gentle
grade of foreign-accent feigning. I consider it a sign of
weakness, not syllabic-sympatico. Dialect-donning takes
advantage of only the crudest, most recognizable traits of the
alter-patter, while making an abomination of the subtle and
more challenging dialectical-deliverance. Moreover, it denies
the whole experience of the person who came by that speech
pattern honestly. I recognize and know the signs of

grammatimorphing onset and regularly witness it as my husband becomes Italian, East Indian, Croatian, or Australian in sixty seconds or less."

Some wordies asserted that the ability to **imitalk** had served them well in their professional lives. Many years ago, J. D. Gravenor of Montreal worked as an operator at Bell Canada's international telephone exchange. This was long before the days of direct dial, and the operators tried hard to connect parties who had limited English or French with their distant families and friends. "Sometimes the less patient operators gave up on callers who were hard or almost impossible to understand. I was one of the reliable 'go to' operators who had a knack for understanding the accents and communicating with the callers. My secret was, obviously, to speak slowly. When that was inadequate, I would lay on an accent that mirrored their own. I became quite good at it, and using this method of 'translating' information, I could connect them right away. I liked it when I was called on to do this part of my job. Even now, if I'm stopped on the street by someone who struggles along in English with a foreign accent, I sometimes fall into my old ways. Maybe this is helpful, or maybe they judge me to be a real sympologue."

Datastrophe

Noun:

the sudden erasure of all your computer work.

Submitted by Craig Chambers, Calgary

Now here's a word we didn't need until the computer came along to make our lives easier and more efficient. Cast your mind back for a moment to the days when typewriters roamed the earth. What was the worst thing that could happen to that piece of paper you were working on? Maybe you'd spill some coffee on it. Maybe it would rip as you were removing it from the carriage. Maybe the cat would walk on it. The point is, all of those things were annoying, but at least you knew what had gone wrong! And you lost only that one page, not your whole damn project.

These days, a **datastrophe** can wipe out weeks of work and bring on that nauseating feeling of loss and loathing that accompanies the click of no return — that human error or computer glitch that is all too often followed by the message "You have performed an illegal action." Oh yeah? Well, show me the law I just broke! Last time we checked, law-making was the responsibility of elected leaders, not those code-writing geeks at Microsoft.

This gap in the language was spotted by Heidi Mack and Rosa Paliotti of Ottawa, and we hope we can all feel a little bit better now that we've named the agony of delete.

- **billgatesed** — Graham Muirhead, Jordan, Ontario
- **blackholed** — Terry Lee, Thunder Bay, Ontario
- **catextrophe** — Hoi Kong, Montreal
- **Darth Voider** — Lillian Hickman, Vancouver
- **datanausea** — Bob Cassie, East St. Paul, Manitoba
- **geek tragedy** — Bethe Wettlaufer, Woodstock, Ontario
- **glitched** — George Bruce, Scarborough, Ontario
- **glurped** — Shayna Kravetz, Toronto

- **manuscrapped** — Pam LeBlanc, Kingston, Ontario
- **manustripped** — Bill Burton, North Bay, Ontario
- **megabitten** — Chris Burton, London, Ontario
- **megawyped** — Craig Livesey, Toronto
- **ramnausea** — John Upper, Kingston, Ontario
- **ramnesia** — Eric Johnsen, Waasis, New Brunswick
- **screenmare** — Maren Goos, Sherwood Park, Alberta
- **typeout** — Mike Lambert, Ottawa
- **wordwiped** — Deb Calderon, Vancouver

When **datastrophe** strikes, the feelings of frustration
and loss can be intense. For some, only the arts can lessen
the misery, help make sense of the **geek tragedy**. That's
when you reach for haiku like these, which have long been
making the rounds of the Web:

> *A crash reduces*
> *Your expensive computer*
> *To a simple stone.*
>
> *Serious error.*
> *All shortcuts have disappeared.*
> *Screen, mind. Both are blank.*
>
> *First snow, then silence.*
> *This thousand-dollar screen dies*
> *So beautifully.*
>
> *Three things are certain:*
> *Death, taxes, and lost data.*
> *Guess which has occurred?*

Dinnerloper

Noun:

the uninvited diner who routinely shows up
at mealtimes, looking for some home cooking.

Submitted by Jim Bowering, Oliver, British Columbia

Let's get this straight. Dinner guests come in two varieties: the ones you invite, and the ones you don't. The second category also breaks down nicely into two groups: the *schnorrer*, a Yiddish term for the **persona nosh gratis** who mooches meals, and the **dinnerloper**, who is an unexpected but welcome guest. It's true that **dinnerlopers** seem to possess salivary glands that border on the psychic, but they are usually good meal companions. They add to the chit-chat and banter around the table. They may eat lightly or heartily, and — we can't stress this enough — they have been known to help with the washing-up.

Ranald MacFarlane of Fernwood, Prince Edward Island, admits to being a **suppertunist**, and defends the practice on cultural grounds. "I have been adopfed into many caring and generous families on the island. My girlfriend is 'from away,' and was mortified when we up and sat down for Sunday supper at one place. I am a dairy farmer and am privileged to come from a culture where if you are there at lunchtime, you are there for the meal. This puts the 'culture' in agriculture. Certain holidays are planned around visits to my adopfed families. Mother's Day means head out to lot 16 for a lobster feed with the Campbell clan. New Year's means my best friend's mother's place. Over the years, I have been their sixth kid. Christmas dinner tends to rotate. If pressed, I would have to describe myself as a major food groupie."

Dinnerlopers can wear out their welcome, but the etiquette for handling this awkward situation is unclear. Here's one way of dissuading **platecrashers** once and for all, proposed by Daniel Terry of Denman Island, British Columbia: "I once read in a newspaper column a story about a woman who wanted to deter a chronic wannabite from showing up at her door. She served dinner and afterwards put all the dirty dishes on the floor for her dog to lick clean. Then, in full view of the wannabite, she put them back in her cupboards. The guest was disgusted and never returned."

Whether you're feeding him or trying to poison him, the **opporchewnist** now has a name:

- **cheapsteak** — Keith and Anne Gorman, Stanley, New Brunswick
- **feedloader** — Len Walbourne, St. John's
- **fooch** — Grade 8 Class, Winkler Elementary, Winkler, Manitoba
- **foodloader** — Mark Adams, Tulita, Northwest Territories
- **mealmoocher** — Jack Norie, Summerland, British Columbia
- **meatloafer** — Sue Batchelor, Kelowna, British Columbia
- **moochaterian** — Mary Ann Mongeau and Toby Harper, Montreal
- **moochivore** — Rod Potter, Richmond Hill, Ontario
- **munch-kin** — Jim and Margaret Anderson, Victoria
- **opporchewnist** — Margaret Ouwehand, Kitimat, British Columbia
- **opportunivore** — Anne Gillespie, Vancouver
- **persona nosh gratis** — Paul Tillotson and Pat Johnson, Vancouver
- **piggysnacker** — Phil McCausland, London, Ontario
- **platecrasher** — Elizabeth Nizalik, Ottawa
- **polterguest** — Mary and Paul Monteith, Kitchener, Ontario
- **potlucker** — Ross Verner, Peterborough, Ontario

- **souplicant** — Alec Kitson, Everton, Ontario
- **suppertunist** — Patrick Artibise, Grande Prairie, Alberta
- **viseater** — Marc Ferron, Ottawa
- **wannabite** — Daniel Terry, Denman Island, British Columbia

Mary Monteith of Kitchener, Ontario, shared her fond memories of the family **meatloafer**. "One of my most vivid memories of childhood centres around this very topic of the serendipitous visitor at dinnertime," she wrote. "I was the youngest child, and my older brothers had flown the nest by the time I was any age at all, but my youngest brother, Doug, did pop back from time to time for a visit. He somehow psychically knew not just when dinner was happening, but when my mom was making roast beef and Yorkshire pudding. He unfailingly arrived on the days when this dinner was in the oven, and in fact acquired mythic status in our family as 'the roast beef psychic.' Sometimes my mother would purposely make it for dinner when she wanted Doug to come over and visit, knowing that the odds were higher when that special meal was being prepared. My brother now lives in Whitehorse, Yukon Territory, and I live in Kitchener, Ontario, and we haven't seen each other in sixteen years, but I suspect that he still makes a psychic connection to a special kitchen in his new hometown."

Droodles

Noun:

the noseprints, pawprints, or handprints left on windows
by animals or children.

Submitted by Michele Kazakos, Welcome, Ontario

When Tracey and Michael Kampen of Port Alberni, British Columbia, suggested this word search, we were sceptical. That instantly recognizable swath of gack on the windows of cars and minivans needed a name, but we didn't relish wading through a week's worth of bodily fluids to get to it. Holding us back was our deep fear of saying "snot" in public. The reward, however, would be the word itself — we knew we shouldn't deprive the language of some new coinage just because we're too uptight to mention mucous.

Droodles are more than just phlegm   they could have a little bit of arrowroot cookie mixed in. Whether man or beast, car passengers can't seem to resist pressing their noses against a foggy window and doodling in the steamy tabula rasa.

Some of the suggestions for this Wanted Word favoured one species of mammal over another, although most were generic. Take your pick:

- **cursmudgeon** — Diane Schuller, Hythe, Alberta
- **dog fog** — Jim and Jean Hayden, Fredericton
- **doggieglyphics** — Kris Hickey, Millbrook, Ontario
- **kindersludge** — Amber Boydell, Hornby Island, British Columbia
- **mucuccino** — Craig S. Dow, Fredericton
- **nasalglaze** — Gordon Drybrough, Edmonton
- **pane stain** — John Marlow, Malignant Cove, Nova Scotia
- **proboscuzz** — Jason Mitchell, Toronto
- **ring around the minivan** — Klaus and Emily Christoffersen, Toronto
- **schmutt** — Marusha Taylor, Qualicum Beach, British Columbia

- **schnozzblot** — Lori Arrowsmith, Barrie, Ontario
- **schnozzogram** — Shirley Hill, Cobden, Ontario
- **slobberography** — Robert Martin, Windsor, Ontario
- **smoodge** — Mike Strothotte, Nanaimo, British Columbia
- **snart** — Andrew Shuller, Granton, Ontario
- **snerge** — Karen Shakleton, Gagetown, New Brunswick
- **snogma** — Rick Nixon, Waterloo, Ontario
- **snool** — Rob Heighington, Toronto
- **woodles** — Judy and Kyle Ferguson, Regina

According to several listeners, these **snot spots** are not
limited to dogs and kids. Here's a letter from Kaili Beck of
Sudbury, Ontario: "This challenge reminds me of something
my friend Karen experienced while driving through the
African Lion Safari in Southern Ontario. The baboons
attempted to leave their mark on the vehicle, but the biggest
and most persistent marks were left by the giraffes. After
much exertion and elbow grease, Karen resorted to the use
of CLR to get the giraffe saliva off the windows. My husband,
Paul, and I had a similar experience with the Safari's eland —
some sort of distant relative of the elk, I believe."

Eyenertia

Noun:

a symptom of exhaustion whereby you stare blankly
at an object without really registering what it is.
Submitted by Adrian Shewchuck, Montreal

You're tired — no, that doesn't begin to describe it —
you're wiped, zonked, whacked. Your brain has shifted
into neutral, unable to absorb any more data. You notice a
calendar hanging above your desk or bend down to tie your
shoelace. Half an hour later, you're still there, staring at that
date on the calendar or that errant shoelace. You are suffering
from **eyenertia** — a trance-like state, brought on by total
exhaustion, that renders you incapable of shifting your gaze
away from the trivial object you have locked on to.

Just about anyone can find himself **mesmereyed** at some
point. A famous painting from the Second World War depicts
American soldiers looking **zombeyed**. That painting is called
The Two Thousand Yard Stare.

The fine-art connection continues with this letter from
Michelle Hebert of Saint John, New Brunswick, who wrote
in with a story about her father, who was a painter: "Many
times following our evening meal, we would observe him in
the transfixed state you describe. Perhaps it was part of his
creative process. Thinking ourselves rather witty, we would
call him Van Gawk."

But perhaps no one is more likely to be **oculocked**
than the overworked, overtired parents of young children.
Karen Thompson of London, Ontario, wrote to us about a
supermom from New Glasgow, Nova Scotia, who had a clever
term of her own for this phenomenon. "It's called 'pausing
for station identification.' It was christened this by my friend
Donalda Moran, who was a single parent of six. She also
attended university and coordinated a second-stage housing
facility for battered women! In her 'spare' time, she chaired
committees, made oatcakes for all who asked, and did a

tremendous amount of running errands for those who did not have cars — all that in between writing papers, making meals, and providing a shoulder for us women friends to cry on. She was, in a word, extraordinary. Whenever she slipped into this daze, she explained it as 'pausing for station identification.'"

Have a look at our wonderful short list. It is guaranteed not to make you **stare-struck**:

- **catagooglia** — Patricia Smith, Sudbury, Ontario
- **comadoze** — Holly Langford, London, Ontario
- **daze-gaze** — Doug Scammell, Lower Queensbury, New Brunswick
- **deep peep** — Jeanette Hashen, Sydney, Nova Scotia
- **dozone** — Blaine Anderson, Goderich, Ontario
- **eyesomnia** — James Chivers-Wilson, Edmonton
- **eyeswidestuck** — Jerry Miner, Wolfville, Nova Scotia
- **glue-view** — A. Du Bois, Dolores, Colorado
- **gluecoma** — Tim Storey, Cormac, Ontario
- **hocus-focus** — Mildren Yeomans, Sisson Ridge, New Brunswick
- **looklock** — Harriet and Irving Brown, Sequim, Washington
- **mesmereyed** — Mary Jenkins, Winnipeg
- **oculock** — Bert and Megan Allsopp, Vancouver
- **semicoma** — Marilyn Lerner, Toronto
- **shark eyes** — Gilbert MacIntyre, Sydney, Nova Scotia
- **staralysis** — Mark Christie, Calgary
- **stare-struck** — Donna Plaxton, Saltspring Island, British Columbia
- **stunspot** — H. Grant, Uxbridge, Ontario
- **zombeye** — Gerald Myslik, Sudbury, Ontario

Fakeover

Noun:

an attempt to hide holes and stains in walls and carpets by rearranging furniture; usually done just before company arrives.
Submitted by Everett Gillard, Grand Falls–Windsor,
Newfoundland

There's nothing like a dinner party to inspire some home improvements. Invite some family and friends over to the house, and suddenly the crack in the ceiling looks a lot more imposing, the burn in the carpet a lot scarier, and the hairballs in every corner a lot more noticeable. It's time for a serious **placelift**.

Why do we engage in these **fakeovers**? In large measure, it's simple vanity and pride. Combine that with the pressure of a deadline, and you can do some major **cosmetic purgery** in a short period of time. Move the rocker over that stain for a little **maskchaira**, do a little **switchcraft** on the paintings and the photos, and — voilà! — your house has been **marthacized** in a matter of moments.

Trish Heidebrecht of Goderich, Ontario, who admits to practising **feng shame** on a regular basis, wrote, "I am prone to episodes of retrofit madness whenever significant company is due to visit. I have been known to decide to repaint the kitchen, wallpaper, and resurface cabinets the day before visitors arrive — usually on a fifty-dollar budget. My worst moment, or perhaps crowning achievement, depending on your perspective, was the day I laid the last floor tile as the doorbell rang. But it is my mother's visits that give rise to this hysteria in its keenest form. I suddenly see my home through her eyes, and although she is the kindest, and least judgmental, of mothers, I know how she keeps her house in comparison with mine. So the day before she is due to arrive, my family is subjected to my mad attempts to upgrade the entire house within hours. This domestic surgery therefore led me to contemplate two medical terms: placelift and a mommytuck."

Our thanks to Davida Glazer of Toronto for suggesting this challenge. Here are some other words to choose from:

- **cosmetic purgery** — Ken McDonell, Ottawa
- **couchmetician** — Leif Bednar, Toronto
- **decoflage** — Margaret Sutherland, Brooklyn, New York
- **feign shui** — Murray Lee, Calgary
- **feng shame** — Stephen Kinley, Guelph, Ontario
- **furniflage** — Paula Silver, Thornhill, Ontario
- **hidey-up** — Karen Nesbitt, Dollard-des-Ormeaux, Quebec
- **inferior decorating** — Neil Graham, Warkworth, Ontario
- **marthacizing** — Brent Flink, Surrey, British Columbia
- **maskchaira** — Ron Butler, South Slocan, British Columbia
- **messquerade** — Maurice Hogue, Winnipeg
- **placelift** — Trish Heidebrecht, Goderich, Ontario
- **remuddelling** — Ken Fraser, Toronto
- **renevasion** — Jim Hutcheson, Wakefield, Quebec
- **renofake** — Ken Summers, Minasville, Nova Scotia
- **renoflage** — Bob Steinberg, Dugald, Manitoba
- **sneaky clean** — Doug Collyer, Toronto
- **switchcraft** — Doug Collyer, Toronto
- **ulterior design** — Mary Delaney, Brougham, Ontario

How could we resist the enthusiasm of Mary Delaney of Brougham, Ontario, who has a long history as a **renofaker**? "I'm so excited, I'm so excited!" she wrote. "I always listen with delight to the words your listeners send in, and despair inwardly that I can never think of one until it's too late. But this time it finally happened! A word sprang into my mind as I listened to this week's challenge while sanding the wall I had just patched with Polyfilla. For the past twenty years, I have been covering this hole with Scotch Tape and hiding that behind a flour canister. You see, I live in an old farmhouse and have neat-o-holic in-laws. Therefore I have practised the art of ulterior design for two decades!"

Isn't this a bit like Potemkin villages? some listeners wanted to know.

Yes, it is, and the verb "to potemkinize" was suggested by several wordies. The villages referred to are those supposedly built by Grigori Aleksandrovich Potemkin (1739–1791), the Russian army officer and politician who was the lover of Catherine the Great. His apparent habit of erecting fake villages in Ukraine and the Crimea when Catherine came to town has made him the patron saint of **renofakers** everywhere. Hence the current meaning of the term "Potemkin village" — a pretentiously showy or imposing façade intended to mask or divert attention from an embarrassing or shabby fact or condition.

Lastard

Noun:

a person who refuses to refill or
reload containers of food and beverages
or toilet-paper rolls.

Submitted by Dan Byrnes, Creston, British Columbia

One of the most successful advertising slogans of all time celebrates a particular brand of coffee that is "good to the last drop." This motto is the battle cry of **lastards** everywhere, people whose enthusiasm for dregs and crumbs is applied to a full range of consumer goods. Many recognize their handiwork in the milk or juice jug that's left with just three drops; the ice-cube tray put away with only one cube; the jar of hardened jam, honey, or mayonnaise returned to the fridge; the cracker package or cookie bag containing half a biscuit; and of course, everyone's favourite, the toilet-paper roll with a single sheet of dangling two-ply.

The **fillistine's** impulse to conserve is a good one, but when the amount left behind is too small to use, he's just being a lazy **lastard**, someone who is avoiding the chore of, say, changing the milk bag. Do you see the difference? I can see the difference. Now let's take a closer look at the short list:

- **dregdevil** — Paul Vandeur, Meadow Creek, British Columbia
- **dregonian** — Terry Day, Newmarket, Ontario
- **fillistine** — Marilyn Lerner, Winnipeg
- **forgetfillness** — Vince and Emily Rempel, Swift Current, Saskatchewan
- **the jug jerk** — Andrea Marshall, Olds, Alberta
- **lactose delinquent** — Charlie Cummings, Toronto
- **lactose incompetent** — Charley Vaughan, Dartmouth, Nova Scotia
- **lazy-faire** — Michele Sullivan, Montreal
- **measler** — Nick Furgiuele, Bognor, Ontario
- **milkbag letdown** — Jane Sly and Jennifer Nelson, Ottawa

- **refillannoia** — The Schellenberg Family, Hepburn, Saskatchewan
- **refillibuster** — Andrea Warner, Terrace, British Columbia
- **refillophobe** — Ken Babich, Saskatoon
- **replacenik** — Eric H. Detchon, Shawnigan Lake, British Columbia
- **secondlaster** — David Odell, Orillia, Ontario
- **task evasion** — Joanne Davidson, Regina

Not all **lastards** are lazy, however. Some of them are just darn thrifty. Take, for instance, the tale one wordie sent us about his Scottish grandmother and her Christmas cake recipe, which called for "one cup of alcohol." The old girl drained her booze bottles of their last drops by standing them on end for a few days. The residue in the cap would then be scraped out and collected in a jar. By the end of the year, she would have the one cup required for her cakes. Anything but a **lastard**, Granny was just being clever and thrifty. And most important, she took care of those last few drops herself, never leaving the chore for someone else.

Leaderhoser

Noun:

a Canadian who, labouring under seasonal denial,
wears shorts in very cold weather.

Submitted by Rick Nixon, Waterloo, Ontario

We all know one — the rugged **leggsibitionist** who takes pleasure in jumping the gun on fair-weather fashions. **Baredevils** can be seen in other countries, but only **leaderhosers** live above the forty-ninth parallel. Their golfball-sized goosebumps and blotchy skin can be seen from coast to coast — at work, in parks, at home. They wander through slushy streets in open-toed sandals, oblivious to the fact that the rest of the world is still shivering through that last blast of winter known as Indian bummer (see *Wanted Words*, vol. 1).

The question remains — why do they do it? Are their internal thermostats broken? Are they blessed with nuclear metabolism? Or are they selflessly offering their frozen flesh to the warm-weather gods for the benefit of us all?

Graham Muirhead lives in Southwestern Ontario and has had the opportunity to ponder the motivation of the **leaderhoser** at close range. "Jordan, Ontario, is such a small town that one nut like this represents a fair percentage of the population. And we do have one. He works at a winery and stops at the local Tim Hortons every morning for coffee. He seems like a nice fellow — quite pleasant, actually — and other than this strange habit of wearing summer clothes in winter, he acts quite normally. But when you see him, as I did just a couple of weeks ago, shovelling snow in shorts, a T-shirt, and sneakers, you have to know something is terribly wrong. I think he might be thermodemonic."

Whether he's driven by wishful dressing or pure eccentricity, the **leaderhoser** is nameless no longer. Feast your eyes on this spectacular list of possibilities:

- **baredevil** — Edith Granter, Rocky Harbour, Newfoundland
- **blukneeser** — Jim Livingston, Lake Charlotte, Nova Scotia
- **brrrrmuda shorts** — Bill Whitehouse, Sudbury, Ontario
- **cooligan** — Rick Solda, Niagara-on-the-Lake, Ontario
- **dressed to chill** — Mike Grimshaw, Vancouver
- **early bloomer** — Jenny Ryley Levitt, Toronto
- **goosebumpkin** — Doug Maloney, Bay Bulls, Newfoundland
- **leaderfrozen** — Steve Manning, Pickering, Ontario
- **leapshorts** — Judy McFarlane, Vancouver
- **leggsibitionist** — Jim Hutcheson, Wakefield, Quebec
- **leiderhopin'** — Rosie Moore, Vancouver
- **pantaloony** — Chris McMahen, Armstrong, British Columbia
- **premature deslackulator** — Laura Cowell, Toronto
- **shivorting** — Margaret Hopkinson, Regina
- **solar bear** — Maggie Duke, Toronto
- **spring equijox** — Glen Dias, Stratford, Ontario
- **sun wishipper** — David Weir and Beth Knowles, New Maryland, New Brunswick

For many, the word **leaderhoser** carries with it strong hints of our national character. Lynda Grandbois of Alberta explains how in this story about hiking with her mate in British Columbia's Glacier National Park. "We were novices, but what we lacked in expertise we made up for in enthusiasm. As soon as we spotted a trail head, we set off in our shorts and T-shirts. The trail rose steeply, and we began to notice that descending climbers were dressed in fancy hiking attire, with trendy boots and walking poles. Undaunted, we hiked on! The temperature dropped steadily as we stubbornly plodded on to reach our goal. When we finally arrived at the peak, 8,000 feet above sea level, the temperature was minus one. There we stood, sweating and shivering. A Gortex-clad American stared at us, aghast. 'Aren't you guys cold?' We just smiled and replied, 'We are Canadian. And we are a hardy bunch.'"

The last word is reserved for Sheldon Mitchell, a **baredevil** from Mahone Bay, Nova Scotia. "I am one of those folks who gives up shorts reluctantly in November and dons them again with glee in early spring. In fact, I wear shorts indoors all winter long. Due to my metabolism, I am warm almost all the time. This has me opening windows and disrobing as much as decency will allow. Because I am warm, or downright hot, most of the time, I am often left panting or breathless. Therefore, my choice of a word to describe myself, and anyone else with this condition, is 'hotpanter.' Many of us are in shorts for this reason, and not because of an exaggerated sense of exhibitionism."

Malapopism

ALL WE ARE SAYING... is "GIVE JESUS PANTS."

SNAP. SNAP.

Noun:

lyrics that are often misheard and then sung incorrectly.

Submitted by Katie Diotallevi, Mitchell, Ontario

Malapopisms are mistaken music lyrics that rarely make sense but fit together sonically. Think of that renowned ladies' man Jimi Hendrix singing "'scuse me while I kiss this guy."

Malapopisms are created by people who don't let missing or nonsensical lyrics get in the way of their own singing enjoyment. They have been known to sing, "All we are saying is give Jesus pants," even though John Lennon was trying to "give peace a chance." Or they sing along to the Rolling Stones' "Beast of Burden" with this merry chorus: "I want to be your pizza burnin'."

Some people will never know they suffer from **lyricosis**, and for them, ignorance is truly blissful. For others, the moment when that ignorance is laid bare is fraught with embarrassment and humiliation. When this **humonymous** reckoning occurs within earshot of family members, the resulting teasing from brothers and sisters can linger for decades. Pity the poor sibling who had the misfortune to sing, "There's a bathroom on the right" to Creedence Clearwater Revival's "Bad Moon Rising."

We like the word **malapopism**. It is not tied to one mouldy oldie and therefore should have a longer lexicographical shelf life. Besides, it is a brilliant reminder of Mrs. Malaprop, the infamous prose mangler from Richard Sheridan's play *The Rivals*. But if that word doesn't do the trick for you, take your pick from these alternative coinages:

- **aphrasia** — Patti Brace, Sudbury, Ontario
- **blunderbusk** — Mike Grimshaw, Vancouver
- **croonerism** — Chris McMahen, Armstrong, British Columbia
- **disclexia** — Terry Hall, Gander, Newfoundland

- **dislyrica** — Tracey Wade, Sackville, New Brunswick
- **ditty-dumb** — Wendy Rodgers, Kitchener, Ontario
- **earlusion** — Gillian Mclennan, Vancouver
- **humonym** — Rod Potter, Richmond Hill, Ontario
- **lipsunk** — Jim Wyatt, Innisfail, Alberta
- **lyricosis** — Sandra Waines, Huntsville, Ontario
- **malapopism** — Katie Diotallevi, Mitchell, Ontario
- **misunderstanza** — Eric Reardon, Waterloo, Ontario
- **singawrong** — Gayle Bulbeck, Neidpath, Saskatchewan
- **slipsync** — Craig Render, Kelowna, British Columbia
- **substitune** — Dean Chatterson, Kimberley, British Columbia
- **tune deaf** — K. Thomas Diotte, Edmonton
- **unclyric** — Terry Noble, Hastings, Ontario
- **vocoloco** — Jeff Smith, Stouffville, Ontario

This Wanted Word was requested by the Carboy Junkies of Renfrew, Ontario. We agreed that it was an unsightly gap in our lexicon, and one in desperate need of filling. But no sooner had we launched the challenge than an avalanche of well-informed e-mail and letters poured in from listeners. Turns out there already is a word for misheard lyrics — mondegreen. This term was coined by Sylvia Wright, a *Harper's* magazine columnist who confessed to mishearing the lyrics of a Scottish folk song popular in the 1950s. The original version goes like this: "They hae slain the Earl of Moray, and lain him on the green." She heard it as "They hae slain the Earl Amurray, and Lady Mondegreen." If this **misunderstanza** does it for you, please avail yourself of the term "mondegreen."

With **malapopisms**, the listener is overcome by a need to make meaning where lyrics are hard to grasp or understand.

This has led to some fascinating and hilarious improvisations, catalogued in numerous publications and web sites. Our favourite is kissthisguy.com. Here are some more samples sent in by our listeners:

Right: I believe in miracles. Where you from, you sexy thing?
Wrong: I believe in menopause. Where's your bra, you sexy thing?
    Daniel Star, Vernon, British Columbia (Hot Chocolate)

Right: I want to be your beast of burden.
Wrong: I want to be your pizza burnin'.
    Greg Fleming, London, Ontario (Rolling Stones)

Right: We stand on guard for thee.
Wrong: We stand on God for thee.
    Olga Vandergeest, Toronto (O Canada)

Right: All we are saying is give peace a chance.
Wrong: All we are saying is give Jesus pants.
    Gillian Crouse, Montreal (John Lennon)

Right: Working-class hero is something to be.
Wrong: A working-class heel is thumping the beat.
    Ken Turner, Rossland, British Columbia (John Lennon)

Right: They paved paradise and put up a parking lot.
Wrong: A gay pair of guys put up a parking lot.
    Mary-Ellen Krupiak, Banff, Alberta (Joni Mitchell)

Right: Hold me closer, tiny dancer.
Wrong: Hold me close, young Tony Danza.
    Jeff Pappone, Ottawa (Elton John)

Meanderthal

Noun:

the driver who observes the speed limit until someone tries
to pass him, at which point he turns into a speed demon.
Submitted by Jane Sly, Ottawa

The highway **meanderthal** falls somewhere on the evolutionary scale between Sunday driver and road warrior. He is neither a road-raging maniac nor a distracted phone-using imbecell (see *Wanted Words*, vol. 1). He is simply a slower driver who is passing-aggressive.

It's hard to know why **meanderthals** do what they do. Maybe it goes back to something in their childhood — the youngest in a big brood, perhaps? Whatever is at the root of their **speedmeleon** ways, they will enforce their **mission: impassable** at some risk to others.

Joanne Smyth of Fredericton, New Brunswick, knows the **meanderthal** well. "I drive fifty kilometres to and from my work in Fredericton each day. Much of my trip follows the curving Highway 8, beside the Nashwaak River. The scenery is beautiful, but it offers few chances to pass slow-goers. When I do start to pass these people, they suddenly come to life, immediately finding the accelerator pedal and flooring it. A hitherto rather reluctant driver suddenly transforms himself into Mario Andretti. There I am, in the passing lane, neck and neck, unwittingly engaged in a test of grit. I can usually coax another burst of speed out of my old Honda Civic to get around them, but I call these drivers 'sudden guts.' This tag emphasizes their sudden and extraordinary transformation from sheep to wolves."

- **acceleramus** — Zoe Kirk, White Rock, British Columbia
- **accelerat** — Pamela-Jay Bond and Shannon Hogan, Toronto
- **dragtag** — Catherine Henricks, Westport, Ontario
- **lane-pain** — Gary Disch, Aylmer, Quebec
- **lanearchist** — John O'Byrne, Dublin, Ireland
- **laniac** — David, Gillian, and Janette Calder, Vancouver
- **lollydragger** — Peter Tuhkasaari, Collingwood, Ontario
- **mission: impassable** — Jo Mittag, Victoria
- **passelerator** — Viv Baker, Collingwood, Ontario
- **speed rump** — Pat and Al Pauli, London, Ontario
- **speed sneak** — Deborah Turney Zagwyn, Harrison Hot Springs, British Columbia
- **speed creep** — Murray Sager
- **speeding escargot** — Mr. Arsenault's Grade 4 Class, Balmertown, Ontario
- **speedmeleon** — Theresa Bessette, Delta, British Columbia
- **thwarthog** — Ken Chown, Brandon, Manitoba

Some people admitted to being **meanderthals**, and they offered various explanations for their behaviour. This letter comes from Paul Paquette of Cambridge, Ontario: "Some years ago I loaded all my baggage, a wife, three children, and a dog into a four-cylinder Volkswagen station wagon for a trip to the cottage. The two-lane road was very hilly, and my vehicle not too vigorous. As we neared the top of a hill, the car would slow down to a sluggish thirty kilometres an hour. The only way I could get enough momentum for the next hill was to accelerate full out on the down side.

"A man in a pickup truck was following me. Unable to pass on the slow upward sides, he turned redder and redder as I zoomed down the slopes on the other side. This continued for several miles, until his boiling point was reached and he raced by me, honking and raising his middle finger. My family's life was risked by his action, and my children's education about middle fingers enhanced by the encounter. I proclaim my action that of an accelegrunt, one whose behaviour springs from the inadequacy of his feeble vehicle."

We also heard from lots of people who blamed **lollydragging** on drivers from out of province. Bill Brown is a trucker from Port Alberni, British Columbia, who drives 160,000 kilometres a year on winding mountainous roads. He writes, "I call them '99ers' — they go nine kilometres per hour on the corners and ninety kilometres per hour on the straight stretches. They're usually flatlanders or tourists. I wish I could take credit for this term, but I believe it originated on another CBC show, I think it was 'Richardson's Roundup.'"

Monodrone

Adjective:
the hypnotic style of vocal
droning associated with poetry readings.

Submitted by Sal Mennen, Fort St. John, British Columbia

Monodrone

We're going to blame this one on the fifties. Think beat generation, think coffeehouse, think black beret, think about some self-obsessed "artiste" at the front of the room droning on in **moronic pentameter** about the ugly materialism of modern life. Fifty years later, **indronation** is still a favourite with poets both young and old, from disaffected beats to spoken-word slammers. The lyrical complaints are different, but the **poempous** sing-song remains the same. Perhaps **monomatopoeia** is an attempt to make up for textual inadequacies. Unfortunately, it often makes the poetry even more impenetrable than it already is.

This language gap was suggested by Ellen Liberman of Vancouver, and judging by both the volume and the nastiness of the replies we got, she clearly touched a nerve. We heard from a lot of poetry fans, some of whom confided that even their favourite poets were guilty of **iambic monotony**. Others claim that **indronation** adds value to the stanzas, like a double shot of brandy with your sleeping pills. Choose your favourite from the list below, but please spare us the **highfalutone** delivery.

- **deatherial** — Kelly Adlington, Oakville, Ontario
- **dronetone** — Ian Sheldon, Edmonton
- **flatlining** — Shonagh Merry, Langley, British Columbia
- **highfalutone** — Joyce Johnston, Victoria
- **iambic monotony** — Steen and Charlene Petersen, Gloucester, Ontario
- **indronation** — Vern Yoshida, Nanaimo, British Columbia
- **lulletry** — Stephen Powell, Surrey, British Columbia
- **monomatopoeia** — Brian Lindgreen, Vancouver

- **monotodrone** — Jon K. Loverin, Halifax
- **moronic pentameter** — Philip Theriault, Chester, Nova Scotia
- **poematose** — Christine and Pierre Gagnon, Foleyet, Ontario
- **poempous** — Jen Love, Waterloo, Ontario
- **poet boreate** — Catherine Henricks, Westport, Ontario
- **poetic vicense** — Eric Wainwright, Orillia, Ontario
- **poetosis** — Augusta LaPaix, Toronto
- **poetronome** — Owenita Rogers, Dartmouth, Nova Scotia
- **pre-tone-tious** — Beverly Zaruk, Mississauga, Ontario
- **sollilaby** — June Stockford, Jennifer and Jon Lamb, Altamont, Manitoba
- **thespianese** — Anne Sikstrom, Victoria

Poetry readings: a literary stairway to heaven or a cure for insomnia? We heard from all sides of this debate, starting with Owenita Rogers of Dartmouth, Nova Scotia, who wrote: "Poetry — a subject I love to hate. Being logical and mathematically inclined, I loathed dissecting poems in class. I could never understand the 'real meaning' of a poem, no matter how much a teacher raved on and on and on about those boring lines. Sorry to all

those people who find this insulting, but I suppose I'm a very shallow person for not getting poetry's 'deeper' meaning. Anyhow, I immediately thought of the word 'metronome' when you described the challenge — so my suggestion is 'poetronome.' Hope you like it, because it sure brings back my school days."

Beverly Zaruk of Mississauga, Ontario, defends poetry's virtues while still chiding those who **monodrone** in this letter: "Many years ago I was married to a young, earnest, sensitive, up-and-coming Canadian poet. By association (and because I was young, earnest, sensitive, and supportive), I was invited to hear many wonderful readings by a virtual who's who of CanLit. But for every magical evening spent listening to W. O., W. P., and bp, there were hundreds . . . nay, thousands of hours spent in serious coffeehouses, listening to serious young writers pouring out their serious — albeit limited — revelations. And that tone of voice? That sonorous drone? Anyone who has done 'time' in the Canadian poetry scene cannot separate the sound from the seller . . . why, it is ever so pre-tone-tious!"

Nerdnest

click.

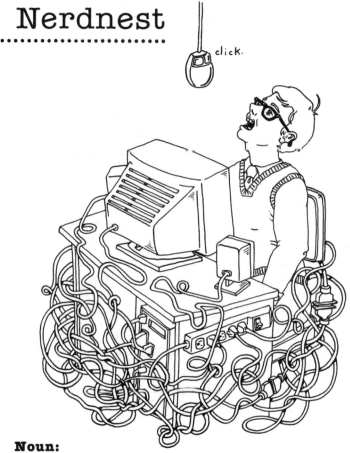

Noun:

the unsightly snarl of power cords and cables
behind computers, stereos, and televisions.
*Submitted by John Farrer, Sechelt, British Columbia,
and Lawrence Wolofsky, Ottawa*

Why does this happen? What mysterious force of nature causes this phenomenon? It seems so simple. You take the AC cord from the printer on your desk and plug it into the power bar on the floor. You do the same thing with the cord from the computer, the cordless phone, the fax machine, or any other gizmo you happen to have. So why is it that all these cords, instead of remaining neat and orderly as they descend from desk to floor, mix and mingle as if drawn together by some magnetic force, and stay that way like a game of Twister that never ends — collecting dust balls and elevating your blood pressure each and every time you try to sort them out?

Miriam Bloom of Ottawa first alerted us to the need for a word for this regrettable by-product of both the home entertainment centre and the computer age. We thought the word **nerdnest** described it pretty well. Here are some of the other wonderful suggestions:

- **cable-d-gook** — Andy McAnally, Humboldt, Saskatchewan
- **cordgy** — Tennille Courville, Westbank, British Columbia
- **cordian knot** — Loreen Martin, Windsor, Ontario
- **corducopia** — Steven Cusimano, Ottawa
- **electropus** — Bob Brooks, Kingston, Ontario
- **jumblewira** — Kitty Edgar, Vancouver
- **plughetti** — Paul Neuman, Sudbury, Ontario
- **powerflower** — Janus Gregorash, Hope, British Columbia
- **progmess** — Erin Stewart, Peterborough, Ontario
- **quagwire** — Denyse VanRhyn, Sydenham, Ontario
- **shocktopus** — Jon Enoch, Kelowna, British Columbia
- **snagetti** — Irvin Cowan, Vegreville, Alberta

- **spaghetronica** — Doug Hicks, Alliston, Ontario
- **techniccini** — Cathy Stephens, Brigden, Ontario
- **wattknot** — Frank Hache, Moncton, New Brunswick
- **wattopolis** — David J. Wilson, Nakina, Ontario

The **nerdnest** is a professional hazard for musicians like George Robertson of Kitchener, Ontario. "A few years ago in St. John's, Newfoundland, I was playing in a band accompanying a musical theatre production," he wrote. "Because we were a rather small outfit — three musicians — I found myself playing two guitars, a keyboard, and a mandolin at various points in the show. This of course meant that I was surrounded by a vast array of power cords, cables, and several effects pedals.

"All was going well until the first act closer, when I reached for my guitar. Much to my horror, I discovered that no sound was coming out of my amp. I looked down at the jumble of cords snaking around my ankles and realized that I had no idea which one was connected to my guitar. I had about two minutes to sort it out before the guitar solo. I felt like Captain Ahab just before he met his watery death, when he got entangled in the lines of the harpoon with which he had speared the great white whale. I fiddled frantically with the cables as the first half of the song became a drums-and-bass opus by default. Eventually I found the loose connection and plugged back in with about three seconds to spare before the solo — which I suppose I would otherwise have had to play 'fabriccato' [see Synchrofake]."

Newbiquitous

Adjective:

describes the experience of becoming familiar
with something and then spotting it everywhere.
Submitted by Kathy Oakley, Halifax

Have you ever noticed something new or unusual, like a new type of car everyone seems to be driving, and then realized that you're seeing it everywhere? That's the familiar newness we've captured and defined in the freshly minted term **newbiquity**.

Here are some examples. You've never heard of the Mexican vegetable *jicama*, and all of a sudden, it seems to be on every menu you pick up. Or you learn a new word, like "prolix," and suddenly everyone's using it. Or maybe it's a trend that you've only just noticed, like celebrities getting nose piercings. Or it could be something well known to all humanity that has somehow escaped your attention, like you've never heard of the Beatles, and now you're hearing their music everywhere. It doesn't matter whether the new concept, name, thing, or brand is known to many or a few. If it's new to you and then seen all over, it's **newbiquitous**.

According to the "experts," our brain cannot take in all the data and information that we're bombarded with in any given day. In order to function, it must absorb information selectively, choosing from among the many details of daily life. **Newbiquity** is what happens when something successfully rises above the threshold of our consciousness, and we are struck by the **coincidensity** of the moment.

Patricia Parsons of Toronto spotted this void, and we thank her for being so observant with this short list:

- **coincagain** — Kim Barker, British Columbia
- **coincicrunch** — Jeff Eyamie, Manitoba
- **coincidensity** — Dan Byrnes, Creston, British Columbia
- **déjà-knew** — Michael DiCola, Ottawa

- **déjà-nauseum** — Sharon Phelps, Lindsay, Ontario
- **déjà-new** — Marshall Tannahill, Geraldton, Ontario
- **divine reiteration** — Doug and Katie, Heathcote, Ontario
- **frecurrence** — Elizabeth Gillies, Chilliwack,
  British Columbia
- **post-cognition** — Ken Dalgard, London, Ontario
- **repiphany** — John Rebstock, Edmonton
- **selectavision** — Joan Lyons, Kamloops, British Columbia
- **trans-ubiquitivity** — C. R. Johnston, Kelowna,
  British Columbia
- **ubiqweirdness** — Annalee Greenberg, Winnipeg

Piggybook

Verb:

to read along with someone else by peering over his or her shoulder.

Submitted by Mike Lambert, Ottawa

Piggybooking is what people do to make a boring trip on a bus or a subway a little more bearable. **Lookworms** will go to great lengths to hitch a ride on someone else's reading material, craning their necks in awkward ways or donning shades in order to appear disinterested. The **parasight** can avoid detection by closing his *eyes* or looking down when his unwitting host throws him a glance. If caught, he risks cruel retaliation on the part of the owner of the reading material — he'll turn the page before the **newsgaper** has finished the article.

Piggybooking is not to be confused with cheating on exams, although these could be considered transferable skills for an aspiring **peeping tome**. And it's not always done secretly — **piggybooking** has been known to happen in the privacy of our own double beds. Most people find it irritating to be on the supply side of an **eavesreader**, but that doesn't detract from our gratitude to Ralph Wilson of Thunder Bay, Ontario, who spotted this gap in the lexicon.

- **cleptomedia** — Carol Wamsley, London, Ontario
- **doppelreader** — Anne Sikstrom, Victoria
- **eavesreading** — Elaine Whelton, Florenceville,
  New Brunswick
- **eyesdropping** — Audrey Hendrickson, Petrolia, Ontario
- **literary vulture** — Janette Freeman, Halifax
- **lookworm** — Peter Powning, Markhamville,
  New Brunswick
- **newsgaper** — E. O'Neill, Fredericton
- **newspeeper** — Gregg and Christine Little, Mahone Bay,
  Nova Scotia
- **overlurking** — Terry Laing, Tantallon, Nova Scotia
- **pagiarism** — Janet Drew, Odessa, Ontario
- **parasight** — Charlie Burton, Victoria
- **peekabook** — Frances Dionne, Jackson's Point, Ontario
- **peeping tome** — Inga Rinne, Bloomingdale, Ontario
- **viewerism** — Bob Butler, Tramping Lake, Saskatchewan

Margaret Hampshire of Terrance, British Columbia, admits
that the craving for reading material sometimes overcomes
her social graces. When this occurs in her household, she
and her husband invoke a strict set of rules in order to break
the vicious cycle of **viewerism**. "My husband and I are
heading towards our eleventh anniversary next month. I give
some credit for the marriage lasting this long to our early
adoption of a set of household guidelines known as the Laws
of Readers' Rights. This decrees that whoever is first to start
in on any reading material can thereafter claim it back at any
time, until they have finished it. Like all legal issues, readers'

rights have been refined over the years. Determining exactly what constitutes ownership of the reading material can be very slippery. The current agreement goes like this:

1. Reading the first paragraph of an 800-page book does not mean you hold the reading rights and can claim it back from the spouse who got halfway through it while you were off on a fishing trip.

2. Being sick with flu, broken limbs, and other pitiful conditions grants readers' rights automatically to the one so stricken. This was amended to include pregnancy, but an appeal to include stupid stapler injuries got nowhere.

"The Laws of Readers' Rights help to keep piggybooking to a minimum, but like slugs in the garden, bookworms can never be entirely stamped out. Just salted."

Proberobe

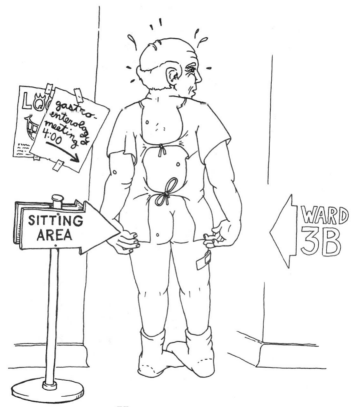

Noun:

the paper or cloth rear-entry smock forced on hospital and clinic patients.

Submitted by Madeleine Adams, Bolton, Ontario

Mention the word "gown" and most people will picture ballrooms, award ceremonies, elegant cocktails. Add the word "hospital" and the picture turns to an elderly gentleman walking down the hallway on his way to an X-ray, his business end fully exposed, like a full moon shining under a harsh fluorescent sky.

Yes, we know, these **cheeksheets** do come with twist ties in the back that are supposed to spare you the embarrassment of putting your buck-naked butt on parade. But really, has anyone ever succeeding in closing the back end of one of these things single-handedly? We don't think so! So you either join the moonwalk or summon an overworked hospital worker to give you a hand. Could this be the reason health-care costs are out of control?

They have been called both the ugliest garments on earth (we wouldn't argue) and also the great equalizer, perhaps because these **flying buttdresses** look equally hideous on both sexes.

They are, of course, designed this way for a reason, which is why we like the word **proberobe**. And depending on which end your doctor is planning to probe, you could be given a robe with front or rear exposure. Carol Stanton, a Vancouver nurse, told us that many patients these days are "double-bagging" as a way to ensure full coverage. We salute those people, just as we salute the clever listeners who gave us this brilliant short list:

- **aftdrafter** — Pauline Boote, Peterborough, Ontario
- **body-bib** — Noreen Janzen, Steinbach, Manitoba

- **bumbersuit** — Ian Walker, Qualicum Beach, British Columbia
- **cape fear** — Headly Westerfield, Hamilton, Ontario
- **cheeksheet** — Michael Ennis, Oakville, Ontario
- **clamshell** — Bryan Black, Medicine Hat, Alberta
- **flapjacket** — Debra Sine, Ottawa
- **flashgown** — Ron McKenna, Dartmouth, Nova Scotia
- **flying buttdress** — Stuart Money, Vancouver
- **gape-drape** — Connie Fekete, Calgary
- **humilidrape** — Tim Coneen, Grand Falls–Windsor, Newfoundland
- **indignightie** — Nancy Telford, Penticton, British Columbia
- **medi-mooner** — Evelyn Doberstein, Spruce Grove, Alberta
- **mooncape** — Alastair Foreman, Vancouver
- **moonsuit** — Allan MacMillan, North Sydney, Nova Scotia
- **oscar de la venta** — Ed Turpin, St. John's
- **paper moon** — Lorene Kilgore, Saskatoon
- **peekabum** — Teresa O'Brien, British Columbia
- **shock-frock** — Harold Gold, Calgary
- **stringcheekini** — Valerie Broman, Kelowna, British Columbia

Rackattack

Noun:

the urge to buy clothes; a variant of retail therapy.

Submitted by Doug Balsillie, Harrow, Ontario

Feeling down? Just heed the call of the mall, fondle the merchandise, and tell yourself you're worth it, baby. The stress and strain of that ungrateful boss just melts away under the warm glow of the track lighting and full-length mirrors. When you're in the throes of fashion passion, you can forget all your problems, forget all your cares, and go downtown for a quick **clothesforce** fix. **Rackattack** is a regrettable urge if you consider how much stuff most of us already have in our closets, but few can resist when it strikes.

This was a popular challenge, but we managed to winnow down the words by excluding some clever terms that craved only specific types of clothes encounters — like serge urge, tweed need, or cotton gimme. Here are some more precious pearls from the fashionista front:

- **clothesforce** — David Darvill, Sidney, British Columbia
- **dressdependent** — Wendy Bell-Stuart, Victoria
- **dressperation** — Neale Van Fleet, Ottawa
- **dresstitute** — Eleanor Pino, Squamish, British Columbia
- **dudbug** — Jeanette Hashem, Sydney, Nova Scotia
- **garmentia** — Terry Laing, Tantallon, Nova Scotia
- **haberdasherneed** — Stephen Brode, Toronto
- **intogsication** — Phil and Mary Beth Toman, Waterloo, Ontario
- **Marcos moment** — Judie Marsden, Stittsville, Ontario
- **melanclothia** — Alison Currie, Oakville, Ontario
- **obsessorize** — Gord Oxley, Toronto
- **sartorial spender** — Leigh Cockburn, Campbellville, Ontario
- **tex-drive** — Pamela-Jay Bond, Toronto

- **tog wild** — Sheila Jeck, Richmond, British Columbia
- **tug-o'-wear** — Gwendolyn Casey, Mt. Albert, Ontario
- **versnachie** — Vern Yoshida, Nanaimo, British Columbia
- **vestmentia** — Ron Romanowski, Winnipeg
- **voguerush** — Josephine Grayson, Toronto

Refrigerot

Noun:

food left to rot in the refrigerator.

Submitted by Jerome Kuntz, Regina

Have you ever reached into your fridge on a hot summer day, looking for that jar of pickled beets, and instead pulled out a throbbing terrarium of turkey and cranberry sauce from last Christmas dinner? Surprise! You just had a close encounter with **refrigerot**.

Until now, you likely referred to these spontaneous science experiments as leftovers. Well, in fact, they're **leftevers** — like that bearded roast pork and blackened lettuce. And what about that green, grey, or blue fuzz growing on top? Why, it's **fridge velvet**, of course. It's enough to give you a **Tupperscare**!

We thank Robin Levy of Vancouver for spotting this void in the language, and we encourage all of you to clean your fridges more often. Here's the short list:

- **bachelor's garden** — Paul Melanson, Toronto
- **crisper critter** — Fred Leggett, Pangman, Saskatchewan
- **fridge fossil** — Cynthia Skensved, Sydenham, Ontario
- **fridge velvet** — Jennifer Seward, Halifax
- **fridgefuzz** — Paul J. Gerroir, Mississauga, Ontario
- **fridgerabilia** — Diane Wile-Brumm, Dartmouth, Nova Scotia
- **fungus bunny** — Marnie MacGregor, Richmond Hill, Ontario
- **grosseries** — Marilyn Wolovick, Kaslo, British Columbia
- **leftever** — Toon Pronk, Fredericton
- **mouldover** — Elizabeth Grace Surridge, Cremona, Alberta
- **petrifood** — Noel Giffin, Vancouver
- **slime capsule** — Phyllis Jacklin, Toronto
- **Tupperscare** — Michael Brady, London, Ontario

The quest for this word reminded Ron Butler of South Slocan, British Columbia, of one very special **slime capsule** from his youth. "I just have to tell you this story from my university years in Halifax," he wrote. "We had a pet salad that lived with us for about eight months. It started out as a nice garden salad mixed in an ice cream bucket, starving-student style. The lid tightly sealed, it progressed, unnoticed, for at least a month.

"When it was finally spotted in the fridge, skulking on the second shelf, no one would open it. It became a contest to see who would dispose of it. Then it stayed around so long that we started liking it. We would feed it our leftovers. I remember stuffing a whole wilted celery bunch, folded in half, quickly into the bucket and slamming the lid. When guests came, we would invite them to view our wonderful 'leftever' through the bottom, much to their horror and our twisted amusement.

"Once, it escaped over the side of the bucket. I was there alone and had to open the lid to sever the creeping tentacle. Inside was another world. Green hills and white towering cities. Grey fuzzy clouds and moist reddish-brown ponds. Something had to be done.

"We decided that burning it was the only sure way to know that it was gone. We took it to a nearby beach and built a big driftwood fire. At first the plastic melted, then the fire reached the contents. Suddenly an enormous two-tone green phoenix rose up from the fire and flew off over the ocean. I should mention that it was March, so still pretty chilly, and we'd had a few hot toddies. I keep my fridge pretty clean to this day."

Refrigerot

Behind (or more precisely, underneath) every stinky scrap of **refrigerot** is a good intention, the frugal attempt to save a morsel for future snacking. But sometimes letting those **mouldovers** rot is the best thing to do, as we learn in this letter from Karen Cookson of Calgary: "I heard a long time ago that Tupperware was nothing more than a fancy coffin for your best intentions. You may as well throw out the leftovers in the first place and save yourself the money on Tupperware. It seemed like a good alternative to the hash my father made us eat for lunch on Saturdays. First, he took all the week's leftovers out of the fridge. Then he ran everything through the grinder, mixing it all together. From roast beef and gravy to macaroni and cheese. From liver casserole to chicken à la king. The resulting mush all got dumped into the frying pan with a can of tomatoes and a can of corn, and boy, it was terrible. Even ketchup didn't help. My sisters and I would beg our friends to invite us over for lunch that day."

Scumberbund

SPLOOSH.

Noun:

the line of dishwater and suds that people
get around their midriffs when they wash dishes.

Submitted by Mark Pidkowich, Vancouver

For most people, taking a bath is an entirely separate activity from housework. But there are folks who somehow manage to combine the two when doing the dishes. They roll up their sleeves and splash around in a basin of dirty dishes so vigorously that when they are finished, they are wearing a sash of suds and scum across their midriffs. Tragically, the **scumberbund** could easily be avoided with that low-tech kitchen item, the apron. Call it the **basin-dixon line**, call it **soap on a dope**, but do try to be kind. This **dishfiguring** wet spot can be the source of considerable embarrassment, especially if the dishwasher is sufficiently tall that the **middrip** becomes a **crotch splotch** or a **sink-dink**.

- **basin-dixon line** — A. S. Fraser, Falmouth, Nova Scotia
- **bulgebath** — Bob Campbell, 100 Mile House, British Columbia
- **bulgewater** — Linda Morris, Welland, Ontario
- **crotch splotch** — Josee Bennett, North Vancouver, British Columbia
- **dishfigure** — Eric Wellington, Stratford, Ontario
- **dishpan band** — Evelyn McNab, Toronto
- **dishtain** — Eric Akis, Victoria
- **high-martyr mark** — Brian Cartwright, Toronto
- **mid-riffle** — John C. Young, Halifax
- **middrip** — Jennifer Smith, Edmonton
- **ribtide** — Shirley McCalum, Regina
- **sink-dink** — Daniel Kraus, Campbellville, Ontario
- **sinkopath** — Phyllis Chisvin, Toronto
- **sinksash** — Nancy Van Patten, Saltspring Island, British Columbia

- **sinksurf** — Marilyn and Wally Turner, Halifax
- **sloshbuckler** — Donna Morrisey, Victoria
- **soap on a dope** — Cynthia Graham, Calgary
- **splashsash** — David and Gillian Calder, Vancouver and Toronto
- **swash mark** — Mike Somers, Port Colborne, Ontario
- **thigh-water mark** — Don Grant, St. Andrews, Manitoba
- **waistwater** — Isabel Fonte, Montreal
- **washbuckle** — Laurie Jestadt, Regina

This letter captures the loneliness and humiliation experienced by one dishwasher, Brian Cartwright in Toronto:

"Dishwashing is, I think you will agree, the ugly stepsister of cooking. It always comes after all the fun of dinner is over, and tends to be a solitary, unappreciated job. All the eaters are rolling about like sleepy walruses in the living room while you toil in the kitchen. You can just hear their conversation and laughter over the rushing water and clattering cutlery — not enough to actually follow

it, but just enough to make you feel sorry for yourself. They go on and on about how fantastic the chicken was. In the kitchen, you're alone, isolated, hidden away.

You don't get the satisfaction of having family and friends gather around, exclaiming, 'Good God! Would you look at the shine on that fork!' And just when you think things can't get worse, you dunk something into the soapy water and send a wave against the back of the sink that then sloshes up over the edge and splashes across your belly. You're soaked, and so is the floor.

"Later, when you join the others, they will stare at your midriff, and they all silently, sadly remark on how you've really let yourself go. In moments like this, you can only cling to the quiet dignity of domestic labour, done without complaint, for your fellow diners. For this reason, I call this holy sign the high-martyr mark."

Showincidence

Noun:

the peculiar coincidence of being subjected
to TV repeats even though you don't watch a lot of TV.
Submitted by Rob Carreau, Antigonish, Nova Scotia

Did you see the *Seinfeld* where the restaurant cook doesn't wash his hands when he leaves the washroom? Or the *M*A*S*H* when Hot Lips and Pierce almost get it on? Well, yeah, I saw them . . . about a thousand times! We know that they made hundreds of episodes of these popular shows. We know that we are supposed to be living in the 500-channel universe. So how come it seems as if every time we turn on the tube, we get not only the same program over and over again, but the same episode of the same program?
Sitconned again! Is this a **showincidence** or what?

The word **showincidence** doesn't take sides on the issue — it merely points out the uncanny timing of repeats.

(Oh yeah, some fluke!) We heard from several people who were grateful for this challenge, if only because it made them realize they are not alone. Wendy Crawford of Errington, Vancouver Island, writes, "This subject is so close to my husband's heart that I called him as soon as the segment had finished airing. He said he was glad to hear that he wasn't the only one who had this form of déjà-view. You see, he has been under the impression for as long as I have known him — fifteen years — that this phenomenon happens only to him."

And here's the completely original, never-before-seen
short list:

- **cee-bee-seen** — Donnie Stewart, Temperance Vale,
  New Brunswick
- **déjà-blues** — Sika Patton, Victoria
- **déjà-tube** — Amy Aikman, Victoria
- **déjà-view** — Taunya Wirzba, Edmonton
- **déjà-vision** — Jeff Parks, Dartmouth, Nova Scotia
- **double vision** — Sheila Donaldson, Toronto
- **Lay-Z-Boy letdown** — Joe Pritchard, Toronto
- **rerundancy** — Sarah Dunsworth, Dartmouth, Nova Scotia
- **rerunnui** — Kate Steger, Montreal
- **seenfeld** — Alan Hunter, Kelowna, British Columbia
- **sitconned** — Gerald Myslik, Sudbury, Ontario
- **stale-a-vision** — Louise Smedley, Tantallon, Nova Scotia
- **teeveedium** — Nancy Mariuz, Ottawa
- **telebummer** — Lea Elhatton, Calgary

David Lurie of Toronto raised an excellent question about
TV programming in his letter. "I frequently got myself into
a lather of expectation in advance of my favourite TV show,
only to be sorely let down by the opening scenes of what
was clearly a repeat," he wrote. "I'm confused . . . didn't last
week's episode close with tantalizing tidbits from 'next week's
all-new episode'? And didn't the network run previews of
the *all-new* episode all week long? What can the network's
excuse be? Did they lose the new show at the last minute?
Did they accidentally leave the tape on the dashboard on a
sunny day? Did their dog eat their homework? This wild

tube-time mood swing, from excitement to frustration, is a two-part experience. Therefore, my word for this draws on both parts of the emotional experience — anticipointment."

While American networks and the Canadian privates may be repeat offenders, CBC Television rarely demonstrates such **teeveedium**. That's not because of its higher calling as a public broadcaster, however, but because it's just too expensive. Thanks to an agreement between the CBC and ACTRA, royalties must be paid not only to the actors of such CanCon classics as *King of Kensington* and *The Beachcombers*, but also to all the musicians, composers, and writers who worked on the show. If you want vintage programming, try your luck on the newer cable stations, which aren't held to the same agreement.

Slamboney

Noun:

the painful poke in the stomach you get
from hitting a snag with your snow shovel.

Submitted by Frank Shinyei, Sandy Beach, Alberta

What's the payoff for shovelling thousands of pounds of snow and ice off a long stretch of uneven driveway and sidewalk? Well, there's the joy of knowing you can get the car out in the morning. And then there's the satisfaction that comes with being a responsible neighbour. In some parts of the country, there's the relief of knowing you haven't broken your city's snow-clearing bylaw. But alas, all too often the only reward that comes from all that hard work is the sensation of being **slamboneyed** in the gut with the butt-end of a shovel. This comes complete with an agonizing stomach spasm and the paralyzing fear that you will never inhale again. Of course, if you're a slightly taller guy, you might be wishing you felt that spasm in your gut.

As Canadians, we know this phenomenon all too well. So why don't we turn this **snowblow** to our advantage and claim it as part of our cultural identity? We could develop the sport of **plow vaulting**, hold national championships, and lobby the International Olympic Committee to make it a demonstration sport in the 2006 winter games. And if we succeed, those sports announcers will need lots of new words to describe what's going on. This short list is a good start:

- **abdominal snow slam** — Patrick Gelinas, Montreal
- **crackhammered** — Stephen Atkinson, Fredericton
- **dishovelled** — Sandra Waines, Huntsville, Ontario
- **drivewaywack** — Etaoin Shrdlu, Montreal
- **implowed** — Jody Willis, Regina
- **ploughman's punch** — Mike Baxter, London, Ontario
- **plow vaulting** — Doug Speers, Summerland, British Columbia

- **pushwacked** — Babs Pitt, Sault Ste. Marie, Ontario
- **shovel punch** — Timothy Sullivan, Toronto
- **shovelectomy** — Marybeth Rubens, Richmond Hill, Ontario
- **snow-belted** — Mike Wassenaar, Rolla, British Columbia
- **snowblow** — Kevin W. Turley, Quesnel, British Columbia
- **snowlar plexus** — Len Wilgus, Toronto
- **snowpoke** — Bruce Wilkinson, Victoria
- **snowpow** — Mark Calahan, Hartington, Ontario
- **suckershovelled** — Jason Northcott, Campbellton, New Brunswick

At the root of every **slamboney** is a hidden crack or snag. Andrew Forber of Mississauga, Ontario, calls these things "zunkers." "I have a zunker in my driveway. It's a surveyor's stake that, despite appearing to be firmly anchored in the ground, seems to move around the driveway. Every summer I take a large hammer and pound it back down into the ground so that its top lies well below the surface. Every winter, as soon as the first snow falls, it slowly rises in the middle of the night, peeks its head above the Tarmac, and lies in wait for the metal blade of my shovel. I swear it's never in the same place twice."

Smolderadoes

Noun:
those groups of smokers who huddle at
the entrances of buildings and homes.

Submitted by Murray MacDonald, Enderby, British Columbia

There's a gaggle of geese, a herd of cattle, a pride of lions — but those sorry packs of smokers hanging around the doorways of office buildings, restaurants, and house parties have, until now, gone nameless. The hardy outdoor tobacco addicts are hereby christened **smolderadoes**. We thought it more appropriate to comment on the pariah status of this **puffoon** than to guess about his health status.

Non-smoking regulations have created these **puffugees**, but apparently not everyone understands what the **cigarazzi** are doing standing outside in the cold and damp. According to several wordies who wrote in, foreign visitors routinely mistake them for prostitutes.

This word search revealed the extent to which the topic of smoking divides us all. It elicited well over a thousand entries, which ranged in tone from the humorous and compassionate to the angry and repulsed. We all have opinions, and some of us have bad habits, but it's hard not to feel a twinge of sympathy for that desperate **smolderado** huddled outside a hospital, one hand waving a cigarette, the other gripping an IV pole.

Matthew Clarke of Waterloo, Ontario, kindly alerted us to this gap in the lexicon, and now we can consider it filled. First, a short list of collective nouns:

- **chain of smokers** — Julie Mills, Kelowna, British Columbia
- **choke of smokers** — Cathy Pelletier, Tottenham, Ontario
- **draggle of smokers** — Dave McBurney, Masham, Quebec
- **faggle of smokers** — Daniel Labrie, Winnipeg
- **fume of smokers** — Arthur Gans, Winfield, British Columbia
- **hack of smokers** — Scott Strong, St. John's

- **pack of smokers** — Emmy Alcorn, Guysborough, Nova Scotia
- **puffin of smokers** — Lynn McIntyre, Perth, Ontario
- **smoggle of smokers** — Douglas Wilson, Clandonald, Alberta
- **sorrow of smokers** — C. R. Johnston, Kelowna, British Columbia

And now, here are some more words from the short list:

- **ashfray** — Mike Jeffries, Moncton
- **butthuddle** — Robert Van Eyk and Corinna Vester, Ontario
- **cigarazzi** — Marianne Hodges, Balfour, British Columbia
- **cigawretches** — Glen Dias, Stratford, Ontario
- **drag queens and puff daddies** — Ron Hooper, Telkwa, British Columbia
- **dragamuffins** — Endl Crane, Prince Albert, Saskatchewan
- **fumadoors** — Carol Freeman, Denman Island, British Columbia
- **fumiclique** — Aileen Gleave, Fort Fraser, British Columbia
- **gaggers** — Chris Marriott, Chelsea, Quebec
- **hack pack** — Terry Bishop, Grand Bay–Westfield, New Brunswick
- **nicoteam** — Patrick Moeller, Saskatoon
- **nicotistas** — Terry Thomas, Saint John
- **phlegmmings** — Meghan Sim, Sarnia, Ontario
- **puffaloes** — Jane Zeidler, Toronto
- **pufflatch** — Helen Kampf, Ottawa
- **puffoons** — Lyn Mattingley, New Westminster, British Columbia

- **puffugees** — Tim Wong-Ward, Toronto
- **smoke ring** — Ken Babich, Saskatoon
- **smokeouts** — Louis Wittorf, Colville, Washington

Teresa David of Ottawa writes: "I know that many people look with scorn upon the smokers who are often huddled outside in the winter cold or soaking up the summer sun. But I have to confess that on occasion, I will indulge myself and steal a cigarette from someone with the sole purpose of going outside to meet some of these social outcasts. I find that I have met the most interesting people in that way, and I know that I might never have had occasion to meet them otherwise."

Sneezebag

Noun:

the person who refuses to admit he's sick, and instead sneezes and coughs all over anyone he comes in contact with.

Submitted by Keith Elms, St. John's

Everyone knows a hypochondriac, that person who claims she can't come into work because, for example, she has a hangnail that might need emergency surgery. The **sneezebag** is the polar opposite. He manages to report for work even when he's hacking up gelatin moulds of bacteria in the lunchroom. **Fluella Deville** doesn't like to give into illness . . . ever. And she has a shelf full of perfect attendance awards to prove it. Her actions imply that sick days are for wimps and layabouts.

A **sneezebag** often justifies the widespread sharing of his viral load on the basis that he is so important the team can't function without him. Of course, it will be hard for these **coughfice workers** to get the job done after everyone else in the company has been hospitalized.

Workplace martyrdom is on the rise, according to Sandra Hoffman, a newly minted couch potato in Ottawa. She writes, "We bought a TV this summer after nearly twenty years without one. We still remember the cold remedy TV commercials that were on in the early eighties. They focused on encouraging people to stay in bed, get plenty of rest, drink lots of fluids . . . and take the advertised remedy. Now the commercials are all focused on suppressing the symptoms enough so that you can still go to work. It has me wondering what went wrong in the past twenty years. Was it a slow evolution to another way of looking at health and work? Why did we all decide that we should heroically spread our germs to all our co-workers? Will this behaviour somehow improve productivity and good relations in the workplace?"

Whatever the **phlegmthrower's** motivation, he can no longer hide behind the excuse of lexicographical anonymity.

Here's the short list:

- **contrachondriac** — Frank d'Ambrosio, Victoria
- **coughfice worker** — Marie-Aline Oliver, Nepean, Ontario
- **coughin' maker** — Norma Cowan, Vegreville, Alberta
- **eagersneezer** — Joy Strickland, Victoria
- **employbot** — Lil Crump, Tantallon, Nova Scotia
- **Fluella Deville** — Jane Davies, Toronto
- **fluzie** — John Archibald, Goderich, Ontario
- **germ of arc** — Teresa David, Ottawa
- **germinator** — Todd Bricker, Dartmouth, Nova Scotia
- **healthnot** — Grace Darney, New Westminster, British Columbia
- **illployee** — Mike McKinnon, Cambridge, Ontario
- **infectivore** — Tim Versteeg, Hamilton, Ontario
- **the office drip** — Tom Trottier, Ottawa
- **phlegmbouyant** — Jeanette Hashem, Sydney, Nova Scotia
- **phlegmthrower** — Marilyn Symons, Calgary
- **sickophant** — Verne Clemence, Saskatoon
- **thermomartyr** — Ann Cornelison, Eastport, Maine
- **working wounded** — Stephen Samuel, British Columbia

Was Typhoid Mary the original **sneezebag**? According to early twentieth-century medical lore, dozens of cases of typhoid fever in New York were traceable to a feisty Irish cook named Mary Mallon. Throughout her deadly career, she worked for several wealthy families and even a maternity hospital, all the time denying she was spreading the disease through the food she prepared. Unlike a **sneezebag** who is visibly under the weather, Typhoid Mary never exhibited symptoms of her disease. She was only a carrier.

Health authorities caught up with her in 1907, hiding behind some garbage cans, and hauled her off kicking and screaming. Quarantined at North Brother Island, near the Bronx, New York, she was released three years later, after promising she'd never work as a cook again. She was unable to make a decent buck any other way, however, and soon was back at the stove, adding a little typhoid bacteria to her preparations. In 1914, she was tracked down and sent back to the island, where she remained until her death in 1938.

Spellingquency

Noun:

the practice of intentionally misspelling
words for simplicity and charm.

Submitted by the Monahan Family, Hampton, New Brunswick

"**M**etaplasmus" is the official term for **spellingquency**, the conscious and selective addition, omission, or rearrangement of letters in words. If that definition still leaves you a bit lost, just picture yourself at a strip mall in Anytown, North America. You buzz the All-Nite E-Z Cash drive-thru teller, get enuf cash for a bagel with cream-cheez-lite at the Kwikee Koffee, then drop by Connie's Cut 'n' Curl Cottage for a trim. Don'tcha just luv the 24/7 convenience of modern living!

It is not hard to see why **funetics** appeals to business people and retailers — **spelling lite** is readily understood and E-Z to remember. As much as the bow-tied grammar police don't want to admit it, **manglish** is a model of effective and efficient coinage. However, this is not a popular position for parents and teachers who are trying to get kids to spell "kwik" quickly. That's why these **bastwords** are regarded as "unwanted words" by many unwelcome interlopers in an already polluted lexicon. The time-honoured controversy over spelling and tradition pits populists against conservatives in a linguistic steelcage match of creativity versus convention.

At the risk of stirring the pot mercilessly, we suggest that inventing and using **phonotics** can be fun. The people who invent these **q-tisms** generally know that they're breaking some rules, but they do it anyway — in much the same spirit that we make up words when they are wanted. **Spellinquents** are not going to let a few rules of grammar get in the way of their creative genius. Like barky one-eyed dogs left behind at the pound, these are the ugly duckling creations of our ever-expanding lexicon. We urge U to adopt a few 2-day!

Infuriating or alluring, this challenge was suggested by Susan Ruptash of Toronto, and here is the short list:

- **appellution** — Kate Steger, Montreal
- **bastword** — Dave Lewis, Dawson Creek, British Columbia
- **cuterize** — Shirley Dorig, Magnetawan, Ontario
- **fauxnix** — Wilson Family, Golden, British Columbia
- **funetics** — Scott Bell, Kingston, Ontario
- **illetteracy** — Kim Marceau, Dawson City, Yukon
- **imbespell** — Lil Crump, Upper Tantallan, Nova Scotia
- **manglish** — Ron Berti, Manitoulin Island, Ontario
- **mcspelling** — Judie Marsden, Stittsville, Ontario
- **or-thug-graphy** — Richard Pepper, Thunder Bay, Ontario
- **phonetic licence** — Maria Edelman, St. Catharines, Ontario
- **phonotics** — Sydney Strong, Quebec City
- **q-tism** — Maureen Hall, Edmonton
- **spellblind** — Lisa Bieman, Strathroy, Ontario
- **spellchuck** — Jim Crane, Prince Albert, Saskatchewan
- **spelling lite** — Brian Martin, Richmond, Virginia
- **spell-wrecking** — Anysia Rusak-Maguire, North Bay, Ontario
- **wordwhacked** — Doris Shields, Ancaster, Ontario

Noah Webster wasn't ashamed of **spellingquency**. Oh, no. He became the godfather of **manglish** when he compiled one of the first authoritative American dictionaries. He simplified the spellings of certain words, dropping letters that he claimed were unnecessary and served only to confuse people. That is why words like "color" and "theater" prevail south of the forty-ninth parallel to this day. For that reason, several wordies thought the term "Websterism" was a fitting bit of coinage for this challenge.

Stufflation

Noun:

a term that describes the law of physics that's in operation when one's stuff expands to fill any available space on shelving, desks, counters, in closets, and so on.

Submitted by Steve Metzger, Hudson's Hope, British Columbia

Back in high school, we were all taught that nature abhors a vacuum. What they didn't tell you is that the fallout of this little-known law of nature is **stufflation**, the uncontrolled spread of junk into tidy clearings and spaces like bookshelves, counters, and tabletops.

Stufflation operates in mysterious ways, which explains why people are surprised to find their brand-new shelving unit filled to the brim within hours of being installed. The same forces are at play when a spacious storage locker is mysteriously filled with sports equipment, tools, clothing, and furniture within weeks of being rented.

It's important to remember that **stufflation** is the expansion of stuff, as distinct from a general spread of mess. The latter is the act of the garden-variety slob, who enters a clean house and leaves stuff lying around until it returns to the state of slovenliness in which he is accustomed to living.

Next time you experience the inexplicable expansion of your stuff into open spaces, take your pick from this modest and manageable short list:

- **brimocity** — Joyce Johnston, Saanich, British Columbia
- **dreckspansion** — Ken Babich, Saskatoon
- **expandamedes principle** — Joe Gaetan, Burlington, Ontario
- **expandemonium** — Robin Frost, Vancouver
- **immaculate expansion** — Steen Peterson, Ottawa
- **junkmosis** — Luke Galea and Jen McAfee, Toronto
- **junkstipation** — B. McKendy, Dorval, Quebec
- **klutteromics** — Bruce Maxwell, Bognor, Ontario
- **packmantics** — Ken Roberts, Toronto

- **pacrativity theory** — Keith Elms, St. John's
- **recumulate** — Bill Ellison, Forest, Ontario
- **stuffocation** — Ms. MacEachern's Grade 7 and 8 Class, Hamilton, Ontario
- **stuffspansion** — Donalda Schindler, Morris, Manitoba
- **supply and expand** — Catherine Henricks, Westport, Ontario

This void in the language was spotted by Marjorie MacDonald of Cranbrook, British Columbia, and as usual, controversy was lurking just under the veneer of this challenge. Some people claimed that there was a perfectly serviceable term already in existence. Tom McLeish McEwen of Manitoba writes: "The term that you seek is commonly known as Parkinson's law. It is named after an English political scientist, Cyril Northcote Parkinson (1909–1993). He wrote many books on history and politics, but achieved wide renown in 1958 with his serio-comic tilt at bureaucratic malpractices — 'Parkinson's Law, the Pursuit of Progress.' In it, he maintained that work expands to fill the time available for its completion, and that subordinates multiply at a fixed rate, regardless of the amount of work produced."

A brilliant deduction, but not quite the same as this challenge, which examines how stuff, not work, expands to fill available space.

Synchrofake

Verb:

to pretend to play instruments while listening to music;
a broader term than lip-synching or air-guitaring.

Submitted by Geraldine Koomen, Kingston, Ontario

To fully grasp the meaning of this word, most of us need look no further than our own childhoods. For some, **synchrofaking** involved the Supremes, a hairbrush, and a full-length mirror. For others, it was a tennis racquet, the rock opera *Tommy*, and the privacy of a wood-panelled basement. Whatever props were used, this process of acting out favourite tunes on fake microphones, drums, guitars, and assorted keyboards was part of a well-balanced childhood. If you happened to miss this critical experience, think *Risky Business*, 1983, and Tom Cruise in his underwear, **synchrofaking** to Bob Seger's "Old Time Rock and Roll."

But here's the catch. While most of us grew out of our passion for **bandomime**, some went on to master the technique and form profitable pop duos like Milli Vanilli. And that's where the hit parade becomes a reprehensible **hit charade**. Rock videos have democratized sham sessions for professional musicians, but it was probably shows like *The Lawrence Welk Show* or *American Bandstand* that legitimized the **dorchestra**.

Whatever instrument you prefer to fake, these words should do the trick:

- **bandalism** — Joan Beecroft, Owen Sound, Ontario
- **bandomime** — Kai Foo, Vancouver
- **bandtriloquism** — Mark Walker, Saint John
- **dorchestra** — Bryn Jones, Aldergrove, British Columbia
- **fabricatto** — Trevor McPherson, Vancouver
- **fauxician** — Dave Pratt, Winnipeg
- **fauxplay** — Brian Sadler, Gibsons, British Columbia
- **hit charade** — Geoff McKay, Kingston, Ontario

- **mock and roll** — Chris Mennell, Cawston, British Columbia
- **mockrock** — Paul May, Vernon, British Columbia
- **perfaking** — Anna Moran, Tantallon, Nova Scotia
- **pseuzician** — Lee Turner, Montreal
- **shake-'n'-fake** — Tim Storey, Cormac, Ontario
- **shamjam** — David Payne, Oshawa, Ontario
- **the Wankin Family** — Paul McKinnon, Arnprior, Ontario

This language void was spotted by Pat Schaubel of St. Catharines, Ontario. We also heard from Joaquin Ayala of New Westminster, British Columbia, who sagely pointed out that **synchrofaking** isn't always a bad thing: "A little while ago at the Vancouver Opera, a near disaster was averted when the soprano singing the role of the heroine in Rossini's *Barber of Seville* came down with laryngitis. With only two and a half hours of rehearsal time, Judith Forst saved the day by singing the part of Rosina from offstage while the original singer acted and lip-synched the role perfectly. The night was a brilliant success, and the next day the critics raved at the singer's marvellous talent and ingenuity."

Mary Robinson of Fredericton recalled her experience with high-school air-bands: "We had an air-band competition every year, where we got together with friends and dressed up like our favourite band. Under the brave camouflage of makeup and costumes, we stood in front of the entire school and danced and 'sang' while the band's music blared out of the gymnasium speakers. I was part of a Devo ensemble that was narrowly beaten out by Twisted Sister — they had access to the wigs in the drama department, but I'm not bitter!"

Yawncore

Noun:

the contagious yawn that is
caused by witnessing someone else yawn.

Submitted by Jeanne M. Davies, Thunder Bay, Ontario

Yawning is contagious. Even thinking about yawns seems to trigger them — you're probably stifling a yawn right now. But why? Scientists believe the urge to yawn lurks deep in our grey matter, and we have little control over it. There's no consensus opinion on why one measly yawn can set off a yawnga line, but here are a few theories:

- It's a primal response that increases the pack's awareness by sending more blood to the brain.

- It's a physical signal that the pack should settle in for the night.

- It signals the beginning of a spontaneous round of Simon Says.

Dr. Robert Provine, a psychologist at the University of Maryland, has studied yawning extensively, and he found that people yawned even when they saw only the eyes and forehead of a yawning face (not the mouth). That's why covering your mouth when you yawn won't prevent a **yawncore**.

This gap in the lexicon was spotted by Doug Reed of Midland, Ontario, and here's the perfect short list to fill it:

- **biyawnic** — Michael Chaiken, Grand-Mère, Quebec
- **chain reactyawn** — Scott Bell, Kingston, Ontario
- **communyawn** — Gloria Neufeld, Ottawa
- **meyawndering** — Dale Benedict, Kelowna, British Columbia

- **phenomeyawn** — Karen Sunabacka, Preston Parsons, and Eric Parsons, Victoria
- **suggestyawn** — Dorinda Smibert, Sylvan Lake, Alberta
- **symbiyawnic** — Gavin Crawford, Regina
- **yawn sequitur** — Mayfair Sign Crew, Chilliwack, British Columbia
- **yawn spawn** — Stacy Doiron, Clydesdale, Nova Scotia
- **yawn-a-thon** — Janice Fincham, Burk's Falls, Ontario
- **yawnference** — Martin French, Victoria
- **yawnga line** — Deirdre McLaughlin, Hinton, Alberta
- **yawnimo** — Don Holmes, Red Deer, Alberta
- **yawnmosis** — Christopher Wilkins, St. Thomas, Ontario
- **yawnnabe** — Marianne Beckstead, Greely, Ontario
- **yawntagious** — Paul Gray, Odenton, Maryland
- **yinyawn** — Laurie Mersereau, Fredericton

Derek Staubitzer shared his sneaky tips for deploying yawns in the workplace: "I have to admit that during 'boring' meetings, I have used this phenomenon to my advantage. I fake a discreet yawn and then watch the yawns begin to rumble around the table. It sends a cue to the boss that the meeting should be adjourned."

One of a Kind

Most of the time, we have to issue a challenge to get a gap in the language filled. But other times, the gap is found and fixed all in one shot. This section of the book offers a selection of the homegrown gems we received this year. We hope you can find room in your vocabulary for some or all of them.

affermation *(noun)*:
the crucial piece of information one receives just a bit too late. "For example, after a good deal of agonizing, you finally purchase a car or appliance or piece of computer equipment, and *then* you spot the consumer report saying what an ill-designed dud it is. Or you persuade your newly single girlfriend to come over to meet the long-time bachelor. You sing his praises, tell her how much she'll like him. As the guy comes in the door, he proudly announces his engagement."
Jill Hill, Picton, Ontario

braxx *(noun)*:
the marks a bra leaves on shoulders. *Dede Boulden, Kitchener, Ontario*

bulligans *(noun)*:
falsified golf scores. *Brenda McDowell, Toronto*

capoodle *(verb)*:
to speak in a strange language when petting small animals. *Audrey Scholtmeijer, Richmond, British Columbia*

carbage *(noun)*:
the accumulated garbage, papers, and other assorted detritus that litters one's car after a road trip. *Patrick Couperus, Ottawa*

carversation *(noun)*:
when two vehicles stop side by side so their drivers can engage in a conversation without getting out. Phenomenon more frequently seen in small towns and rural areas. *Bruce Burrows, Sointula, British Columbia*

fogey tale *(noun)*:
a story of days gone by, told by parents and grandparents to bored but polite children and youths; similar to a fairy tale. *Howard Goodman, Toronto*

keyfuffle *(noun)*:
the action someone makes when searching himself for his car keys in a rather frantic fashion. *Suzanne Steele, Metchosin, British Columbia*

meltifact *(noun)*:
an item that appears out of a melting snowbank (for
example, a shopping cart at the edge of a mall parking lot).
Lisa Thompson, Strathroy, Ontario

moverang *(noun)*:
a person who leaves home, moves all over the place,
and then finally settles back where he came from.
John Thompson, London, Ontario

niblings *(noun)*:
an inclusive term for both nieces and nephews.
Anne Fleming, Vancouver

nopenesia *(noun)*:
the inability to find a pen when inspiration strikes.
Claire Freeman Fawcett, Toronto, Ontario

pee-mail *(noun)*:
the markings and scents dogs sniff at on their rounds. "I have
always referred to this as my dogs checking their pee-mail."
Corinna Meijers, North Vancouver, British Columbia

pubertory *(noun)*:
those years when you are neither child nor adult. "All the
angst, the sense of displacement, the yearning for what is
to come, and the sorrow for what has already gone."
*Chelsea Matisz and Elizabeth Blair-Matisz, Medicine Hat,
Alberta*

reminiscent *(noun)*:

a memory triggered by smells (a.k.a. smellory).
Romeo Graham, Chelsea, Quebec

satisigh *(noun)*:

a sigh of contentment and satisfaction. *Sharen Findlay,
Guelph, Ontario*

scummett *(noun)*:

bad Shakespearean verse. *Dawna Rae Hicks, Toronto*

three dub dot *(noun)*:

an easy way to say the three W's that precede a web site
address. *Verne Dennis, Ingersoll, Ontario*

vulture *(verb)*:

to hover, impatient for dinner to be served. *Laurie Durst,
Kapuskasing, Ontario*

yestertimes *(noun)*:

refers broadly to the past or to particular events that
happened yesterday, last week, or last year. (The opposite
of yestertimes is nextertimes, which can be substituted for
tomorrow, next week, or next year.) *Dwayne Regehr,
Winnipeg*

Did you enjoy
Wanted Words 2?

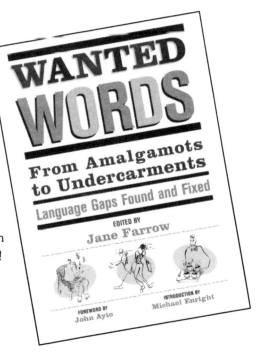

Then you'll
want to pick up
*Wanted Words:
From Amalgamots
to Undercarments*,
the first installment in
this bestselling series!

ISBN 0-7737-6175-6 $9.99

www.stoddartpub.com